ripples

a memoir by:
ellen gilliland

thanks and dedication

I would like thank my friends and family
for their love and support for this project and
throughout my life. Thank you Mandy and Vicki,
for encouraging me to pursue all options to get
Ripples published. I dedicate this book to Greg,
Brian and Ashley; I love you more than you will
ever know. Your faces keep me motivated on the
treadmill of life. To my sisters, Beth and Nancy; I
would have never lived to tell of these events
without our survivor alliance. To my Mother; I
hope you have found rest and happiness with
those who were so special in your life. And to
Dad, Raymond and Julia; each day I wish there
was no story to tell, because that would mean
that your lives had not been severed when there
was so much living ahead of you.

prologue

Every decision and choice that we make as individuals impacts those around us. As I look back over my pilgrimage, it is apparent that my every action, or lack of action, has affected other people. It's like dropping a stone into a lake, sending out ripples that move outward in ever-widening circles.

A drunk driver. A car crash.
A descent into a spider's web.

*As my life and security fragmented around me, I
would struggle to adapt to an unfamiliar world full
of unfamiliar people and unfamiliar surroundings.
Consumed by grief and fighting to survive, my
fractured family sought to re-piece our lives from
the brokenness of our personal and shared
tragedies. Each decision, each choice made was a
stone pitched into the ever-moving waters of our
lives, causing ripples to move into ever-widening
circles around us.*

chapter 1

1958 - 1963

My life ended when I was four years, nine months and seven days old. Up until that point, life was pretty great….

Mom and Daddy were high school sweethearts in Pittsburgh, Pennsylvania. Dad was an overachiever. He had younger sister, and was well liked and respected by his peers. Mom was a real dynamo. As the oldest of four, she loved a challenge and had no hesitations about paving her own way in life. They planned to get married after college, but WWII came along and things were put on hold for a time.

Daddy joined the Navy and was moving all around the country doing his flight training. Meanwhile, Mom applied and was accepted into an experimental accelerated engineering program for women. She completed the two year course at Penn State in just one year, while almost half of the girls in her class flunked out. Because her college expenses were covered with scholarships, her dad said she could use the money he had saved for her college education to get her pilot's license. On the days she was scheduled to fly, she would walk the 5 miles to the airport and sit under the wings of a plane studying until it was time for her lesson. She was one of the first women pilots in the United States. She decided to enlist in the Navy in 1944. She was stationed in Alameda, California at an airstrip where she helped transport parts and soldiers across the country. She was truly a woman before her time.

The war was over in August of 1945, and Daddy took the option of an early discharge. However, Mom was still enlisted. They planned a wedding in one week while she was home on leave in October. They tied the knot on October 17, 1945, but Mom was not discharged from the Navy until November of that year. At that point, like many other veterans, they went back to college to finish what the war had interrupted. They both enrolled in Penn State, and lived in a trailer on campus along with many other newly discharged veterans. Mom graduated from Penn State in September 1947 and Daddy graduated in May of 1948. My brother, Raymond, made his appearance during Daddy's final week of classes – a very special graduation gift.

After college, they decided to settle in Pittsburgh so they would be close to their families. Daddy's parents lived in the downtown area, just a short drive away. His father was a retired carpenter and his mother was a homemaker who made wonderful chocolate chip cookies. Mom's dad was a chemical engineer and worked for the government investigating gas explosions. He designed and patented several coal mine lanterns. It was also his recommendation to add an odor to natural gas to make leaks more easily detected. (Not many people can brag that their grandfather put the stink in gas.) He died suddenly at age 64, which meant that Grandma Jones was widowed by the time I came into the family.

Daddy got a job with an aluminum company in downtown Pittsburgh, and they purchased a three bedroom home with one bathroom and a basement. With four children in pretty quick succession, they soon outgrew this little nest. Mom began designing her dream home and they had it built not far away in a new development. The lot had a steep slope at the back which allowed for a full basement and a backyard that was perfect for sledding and other fun adventures. The neighborhood was filled with families with multiple children, so there was always someone to play with. The new house had a bedroom for everyone plus an apartment for Grandma Jones on the ground floor. Mom designed the house to make life easy for our active family. There was even a laundry chute from the top floor to the basement that provided endless entertainment of sending toys and dolls to tragic outcomes from the long fall.

Mom always said "New house; new baby" and that is where I came into the picture. I was the baby in a family of five – an unexpected surprise you might say. My entrance into this world was less than graceful. While in the hospital's newborn nursery, I contracted a skin infection. The result was that my body was covered with large draining wounds that didn't make me very cute or adorable. It took meticulous care for many weeks to get the infection cleared up. But, my family loved me, boils and all.

Our family dynamics were as follows; Raymond was the oldest and the only boy, eleven years older than me. He was a survivor in this family filled with females. He spent a lot of time hunting and doing outdoor bonding activities with his male relatives. Raymond was Mom's number one lawn care person and helped with other chores around the house. My earliest memories of Raymond are of him sticking his smelly socks and feet in our faces. Our screams always brought a smile to his face.

Julia was 8 years old when I arrived and became my surrogate mother. She was literally Mom's little helper, making sure we all did what we were supposed to do. Beth was next in line, 5 years older than me. She was the easy going middle child. Nancy, who arrived 14 months behind Beth, was the tomboy of the family.

Grandma Jones was also an integral part of our daily lives. She lived with us for weeks at a time, with plans to live with us long-term as she got older. She was always ready to listen to our woes. I was her namesake, which made me feel that our bond was extra special. She would hostess the most amazing tea parties for us and our friends, complete with a real china tea set from England. She would slide her glasses down to the tip of her nose and speak in a perfect English accent, "More tea, Madam?"

But my most favorite person in the world was my Daddy.   As far as I was concerned, he hung the moon. Being a daddy's girl, I would eagerly await his arrival home from work each afternoon. He would unwind in his favorite rocking chair which afforded a tranquil view through the picture window overlooking the backyard. I would do my best to entertain him with jokes and stories. I had a reputation of being a bit of a chatter box. He called me Bebe and if I wasn't beside his chair talking his ear off, then I had my arms wrapped around his leg so I could go wherever he went. When the rest of the family would go to the movies, I would stay home to "baby sit" Daddy. This meant that he would doze on the couch while I would sing and dance around the room entertaining him. He was the sun in my world.

Life was busy in the Gilliland family. Daddy's favorite book was The Little Red Hen and in many ways, this book personified his ethics of life: work hard, don't procrastinate and be dependable. My dad was the Safety Director for his company, which meant he did a lot of traveling. He was also a volunteer fireman for our township. He stayed active in our church and loved to hunt and spend time outdoors. He was conscious about safety in every area of life. His hobbies included woodworking and he created some amazing pieces of furniture for our home.

Mom had to be organized and on top of things to keep our family of seven running smoothly. She had a kaper chart posted in the kitchen with a rotating paper wheel in the center. The wheel was divided into five pie slots and each of our names was written in a slot. The wheel was rotated weekly to a new duty roster, which meant that each kid had assigned duties for that week. Mom was a firm believer in the value of chores and everyone pitching in. She was also busy with activities in the community, the church library, Girl Scouts, Boy Scouts and teaching swimming for the YMCA.

Mom was a real trouper about letting us have pets, and there is a long list of those deceased, but much loved, critters. The most memorable of all of our pets was Beth's cat, Tinkerbell. In kindergarten and first grade, Beth struggled to learn how to read. Mom had tried all kinds of different teaching methods with no success. Finally, one day out of desperation, she told Beth that she would get her the one thing she wanted most in the world – a kitten, if she would just learn to read. It worked like a charm and Tinkerbell became the king of the pets in our home. He was a black Persian cat who ruled the house with an iron paw. No one pushed Tinkerbell around.

I was personally educated to this fact by Tinkerbell himself. As a toddler, I had developed a nasty habit of biting. The pediatrician told my Mom that the best way to stop it was to have my victims bite me back. One day I pulled Tinkerbell's tail, and he promptly bit me. Taking a lesson from my siblings, I returned the bite. Mom was little surprised to find me with black Persian cat hair coating my mouth and Tinkerbell looking very annoyed.

Our family vacations were usually spent camping. Nothing will bring a family closer than spending a few nights together in a tent. Mom kept all of the necessary supplies organized and ready to go. One year for his birthday, Raymond got a Styrofoam sailboat. We soon discovered that not only did it constantly shed Styrofoam, but it also easily broke into pieces. However, these issues did nothing to diminish our fun out on the lake.

Other trips included family reunions at Lake Michigan. Heaven must be like one big family reunion. We would recognize a few faces, see a lot of new faces, and yet feel a connection to them all. These were events with crowds of people that we were somehow related to, but the family roots and vines were too difficult to untangle. The important things to us kids were the swimming, wading, sailing, endless bounty of food and family card games that kept us entertained. We learned early how to play Michigan Rummy and would always play cards whenever a family group was together. It was at one of these reunions that Beth would bond with our second cousin, Donna Sue. They were the same age and there was an instant connection that would last for years to come.

With five kids, there was always a crisis of some kind going on. Mom took these in stride, like a good general. One afternoon, when I was about three years old, Mom was busy setting up the living room for a party. I had sneaked into the room and was eating the peanuts she had just put out. When she walked back into the room, I was fully aware of two things. One; I was not to be in the room she had just cleaned, and two; I was definitely not supposed to be sampling the peanuts. In surprise, I gasped, sucking the peanut right down into my lungs. I immediately went into respiratory distress and was struggling to breath. They rushed me to the emergency room where I had to have an emergency procedure to remove the peanut. When the offending nut was safely removed, I was given an injection of penicillin "just in case." Unbeknownst to us, I was deathly allergic to the penicillin and went into shock. The penicillin caused more problems than the peanut. Needless to say, the dinner party was canceled.

Another injury occurred when I tried to teach my cousin how to play "horsie." I couldn't understand how a reasonably intelligent kid could fail to grasp the dynamics of putting a rope around another kid's waist and running behind them yelling "giddy-up". It was one of my all-time favorite games to play. On this particular afternoon, my cousin was dutifully running along behind me yelling the appropriate terms when I looked over my shoulder to make sure he was holding the reins correctly. When I turned back around, I ran straight into a metal "For Sale" sign on an empty lot.

The metal edge split my face open from underneath my nose through my lip. Mom and Julia calmly loaded me into the car and took me to see my pediatrician and hero, "Dr. David" who stitched me back together so well that today the scar is barely visible.

Our neighborhood was built on a hill with our house situated at the bottom where the ground just leveled out. It was the prefect elevation for sledding and biking. We spent hours pushing our bikes to the top of the street and then flying down at warp speed with the pedals spinning so fast that we had to put our feet up on the handlebars. We were always sporting some type of scrapes or bruises, but Beth had a particularly bad fall from her bike while speeding down the hill and was sporting a broken arm as a result.

Our family was loud, happy and affectionate. There was never a dull moment and we always seemed to have some adventure in the making. As children, we knew that we were loved by our parents, who tucked us into bed each night after saying our prayers. As they gave us our bedtime kiss, they would always say, "Don't let the bedbugs bite tonight." I had no idea what this silly saying meant, but it always made me feel loved and cherished by my big boisterous family.

chapter 2

july 17th, 1963

It was July 17, 1963 and I was four years, 9 months and 7 days old. We were having a family birthday celebration for my dad. He would be turning 39 in two days, and it was the one free night for us all to get together with his parents for a picnic at their house. I took the party seriously and got dressed up in my favorite Sunday dress. (It was green gingham and had a big bow in the back, accessorized with my dress shoes and shocks.) Julia, older and wiser at age 12, gave me a hard time about dressing up when the rest of the family were wearing shorts. Beth, at 10 years old, was sporting her broken arm from her bike wreck. Nancy, our family tomboy, was 9. At 15, Raymond was the only unhappy one with the family party plans. He had to forego a teen social at our church to do this birthday event, and there was no way that a family gathering could compete with the opportunity to hang out with his friends.

We drove our new green VW bus to our grandparents' home. We had only had the van for 5 days and the new car smell was still strong and fragrant. It came equipped with a new safety feature; seatbelts for the two front seat passengers. Our other vehicle was an older red VW bus that Mom was driving separately to the party, so that she and Grandma Jones could run an errand on the way home. Everyone had a great time and we were happy and content when it was time to head home. Grandma and Grandpa Gilliland had given Daddy a bag of play sand for our sandbox as one of his gifts, which was loaded into the back of the van. All five of us kids piled into our seats with Daddy to head home. We were going the more direct route home, which would take us by our church. Mom headed in the opposite direction with Grandma Jones.

Raymond, sitting in the front seat, became gloomy when he saw that the teen party was still going on at our church when we passed by. I was standing behind the front seat singing to my dad. I liked to entertain myself by sticking my fingers between the gap of the front seat and the metal wall behind it. I would try to jerk my fingers out before they got pinched. I was listening to Daddy and Raymond talking about the dance as we started around a curve just past the church. We were only four miles from our home when the world suddenly exploded around us. A drunk driver came around the curve with no headlights on, in a dark car traveling in the wrong lane, hitting us head-on. The impact of the vehicles shattered every window in our van and the birthday gift of sand was sent swirling around in the air, pelting us and filling our lungs.

Daddy was killed instantly, when the steering wheel plunged into his chest and the impact of the crash broke his neck. Raymond was catapulted from the front seat through the windshield when his seatbelt buckle broke. He was run over by a third car that was unable to stop. Julia, sitting in the seat next to the side door, was crushed when the door opened and closed, trapping her. Nancy was airborne from the second seat and crashed into the metal roof vent. She was scalped by the metal pieces. Beth, with one arm already in a cast, was tossed around the van like a rag doll. And I was trapped by my fingers that were pinched between the front seat and the metal wall.

When the noises of the crash subsided, screams and cries for help filled the air. Beth was the only one conscious in our van. The area hospitals had their own ambulance services for transport and responded to the calls for help, but there were just too many victims. Daddy's volunteer fire department was called to help transport the injured. When they arrived on the scene, they didn't even recognize us in the jumble of twisted metal, blood, and bodies. I was picked up by the firemen and transported in the fire truck to the emergency room.

When Mom and Grandma Jones arrived at home, they found a dark and empty house. Mom, sensing that something was wrong, began calling area hospitals to see if there had been an accident. The first few phone calls were unfruitful, as the staff members had no time to waste. Finally Mom called a hospital that asked for a description of the family members she was looking for. She was told they had a young male that matched her description of Raymond, and she needed to come down right away.

Frantically, they drove to the hospital. When they arrived, they were told that there had been a multiple car accident and Raymond had not survived. Mom began to try to find out where the rest of her family was. Her nightmare journey trailed to a second hospital, where she found that Daddy and Julia were also dead, and the remaining three of us were in critical condition. Beth had multiple lacerations and a compound fracture of her left leg where it was broken in two places. She was in surgery for placement of a rod to stabilize it. Afterwards she was put into traction and eventually a body cast. Nancy and I were both in surgery with multi-trauma. The surgeons worked on Nancy for over 6 hours, trying to put her scalp and face back together. One of her eyelids was cut all the way through and her left ear had almost been completely severed. In addition, she also had two broken legs that required surgical stabilization with rods. I had severe internal injuries, a head injury, a shoulder injury and was not responding well. Mom wasn't sure I was going to make it. She was keeping vigil next to my bed when a nurse wearing a nursing cap came in to check on me. I told the nurse to take off her silly hat. At that moment, Mom knew that I had turned the corner.

They would pull pieces of glass out of our bodies and sand out of every nook and crevice for the next several weeks.

The ripples from one person's decision to drink and drive meant that life was forever changed for our family.

chapter 3

1963

I often wonder how my mother survived this wreck and the loss of her family. Yes, three of us survived that accident, but we would never be the same family and each of us would be changed forevermore. Mom was a strong woman who was surrounded by a wonderful support system of friends and family. She had three little girls whose lives were hanging in limbo, as we fought to survive. She also had her faith. But in many ways, Mom was forever changed that night, unable to unconditionally love us after that tragedy. It was as if her heart was broken and she didn't have any pieces left to share.

Mom was a strong believer that when something bad happened, you had to work hard to turn it into something good. While attending our church some months before the wreck, she, Dad, Raymond and Julia had listened to a presentation about organ tissue donation. This was a new and exciting medical breakthrough. People with vision loss due to corneal disease or damage, could have their vision restored by a new procedure called corneal transplants. The four of them agreed that this was a wonderful thing to do for others, even though death seemed so far away.

As she sat by our hospital beds praying, she looked over at Nancy's head and face wrapped in bandages. The doctor had told her that Nancy had almost lost her left eye because her eyelid was cut completely through. As she contemplated his words, she suddenly remembered her conversation with Daddy, Ray and Julia about the cornea donations. She asked Grandma Jones to quickly call the eye bank. Was it too late to donate the corneas from her husband, son and daughter? Were any of the corneas usable? She was told that five of the six corneas could be used for people awaiting corneal transplants. She quickly signed the necessary papers to start the harvesting.

The information about the recipients was supposed to be kept confidential, but snippets of information trickled down through the hospital grapevine. A housewife could now see clearly to take care of her family; a father could now enjoy the great outdoors; a nun who was a first grade teacher could use her eyes to teach the children that Julia had dreamed of teaching some day. Mom's decision resulted in ripples across the surface of these lives.

An autopsy confirmed that the driver of the car that hit us was drunk. He had been at his club drinking, and then climbed into his car to drive home.

He never even bothered to turn his lights on, being too intoxicated to miss them in the dark. He died at the scene.

Our physical recoveries were slow. All three of us were put in the same hospital room so we could be together and to make things easier for Mom. Unfortunately, this meant that I was in a metal crib to allow room for the other two beds. At 4 years of age, I was not happy about this arrangement. I was not a baby and resented the crib. I was also not the best patient. One night the nurse came through to check our vital signs. I absolutely refused to open my mouth so that she could check my temperature. She gave me three chances and when I still refused, she announced that she would go and get the rectal thermometer and be right back. My cries of surrender had no effect on her mission and that was the night that I developed new respect for nurses and the work they do.

In the meantime, Mom had to plan a memorial service for Daddy, Raymond and Julia. Because of our injuries, we weren't able to attend. We didn't have the opportunity to say goodbye or have any closure with their deaths. As long as we were in the hospital, we could pretend that they were at home waiting for us.

After many weeks in the hospital, we were sent home to finish our physical healing. Mom and Grandma Jones worked diligently to arrange the house in order to accommodate us and our medical equipment. We were moved into Grandma Jones' private apartment on the main floor. I was on bed rest in a small bed in the corner of the room. Beth and Nancy were both in hospital beds fitted with traction equipment and trapeze bars.

One day as Nancy was using the trapeze bar over her bed to pull herself up, her arm snapped. This just added one more cast to the mix. Mom probably could have gotten her orthopedic nursing certificate by the time we were up and walking again.

Getting us out of the house was a whole new challenge. Beth was in a full body cast at this point and could only get around in a wheelchair by semi-reclining. She and Nancy would share a wheelchair and pretty much clear the aisles when we were in stores. I was pushed around in a baby carriage as I was still on bed rest due to my fractured pelvis.

The community opened up their hearts to us to help in whatever ways they could. Boxes were set up on street corners outside of stores to hold donations of toys for us. We received everything that was made in 1963 for Barbie and her friends. Family friends, neighbors, church members and strangers came in to help care for us and to entertain us when inactivity became overwhelming.

When the doctors finally said that I could start walking again, I planned a grand entrance – Ellen style. My legs were weak and shaky from lack of use. There was a large group of people over at our home that evening; almost our entire support system. With my sisters' encouragement, I threw one of my dolls into the center of the room, where they were all sitting around talking. No one noticed my first exhibition, so I went back to the door and launched another beloved baby into the center of the ring and walked out and picked her up. Much to my delight, the crowd went crazy. I felt very accomplished in my ability to ambulate independently once again.

That fall, I started K-5. Beth and Nancy had to start the school year in wheelchairs. The entire school grieved with us, because Raymond and Julia had been students there. Teachers would often look at us and start crying. Our status at school had changed. We were now singled out among our peers during a time when we really needed school to be a normal place, because our home would never be the same again.

One day I was playing in Grandma Jones' apartment when I looked up just as a bird flew straight into the large picture window. I ran outside to see if it was okay. It was obvious to Mom and Grandma that it had broken its neck, but I was determined to nurse it back to life. I scrounged up a shoe box and padded it with tissues and gently laid my patient on the soft bed. I carried the shoe box with me everywhere, singing and talking to it. Mom was beside herself trying to convince me to let them bury the bird and put an end to the emotional trauma. Finally I relented, and the bird was given a proper funeral. Looking back, I realize that this was my attempt to understand what death meant and how to deal with it.

I turned five years old, three months after the wreck. Mom's Girl Scout troop wanted to do something special for us. The girls planned a surprise birthday party for me with all of my friends. It was in the game room downstairs in the basement. There were no worries about my stumbling onto the party preparations because I had developed a phobia of the basement after the wreck. I had all kinds of visions of things lurking down there that could cause me harm. Needless to say, my surprise was totally genuine when everyone yelled out "Happy Birthday!" It was a birthday party I will never forget.

Time passed day by day. The scars on our bodies began to fade and the broken bones healed, but the emotional scars would never disappear.

chapter 4

1964

When someone has experienced a major trauma or loss in their life, they must grieve. It is the only way that they can pick up and move successfully through life. If they fail to work through the grief process, they will be crippled emotionally and make poor choices as a result. Facing that grief and dealing with it are the only ways to become stronger.

My mother did not allow herself to grieve. Sure, she cried and wept for the loss of her loved ones and the loss of her family, but she never really let herself grieve. She was holding on by her fingertips to a slippery edge, while trying to put the pieces of her life back together and to be strong for her daughters.

After the wreck, Mom had no financial worries. Daddy had made sure that he was well insured, and there were the settlements from the wreck and the seatbelt company. Mom had sued because Raymond's seatbelt buckle broke in the accident. This lawsuit helped lead to standardization of seatbelts and ultimately helped save lives. Mom got some sound financial advice and set up a trust fund for each of us. It was enough money to get us through college and settled in life when we got older. There were also the monthly social security checks. With careful planning, she would not have to worry about money for the rest of her life.

Because of the newness of the organ tissue donation, Mom was asked to do some interviews and wrote articles for <u>Time</u> magazine and <u>Guideposts</u>. She began to get some response letters from some of her readers. One of the people she began corresponding with was a man from the Deep South. He was an aeronautical engineer and a pilot. Mom's interest was piqued because they shared these common interests. They began talking on the phone and he even flew up to meet her in his private plane. Perhaps a man that shared her love for airplanes and had no ties to her hometown seemed like a good escape hatch from her constant grief. She was a young widow who had been left well taken care of financially by her deceased husband and she was ripe for the picking.

His name was Charles Meagher and he lived in a tiny community called Prospect, Tennessee. He was divorced and had three children. He owned a ranch of about 300 acres with some cattle. He worked for NASA in Huntsville, Alabama, commuting an hour to his job every day. Charles painted a rosy picture of the life of a rancher. Mom began to consider the possibility of escaping from those daily reminders of what she had lost: the house she and Daddy had designed and built together, the football field where Raymond had played ball, the place where Julia had taken piano lessons, the curve in the road where they had died, the church where they had sat as a family.

Everywhere she turned, she was surrounded by reminders of what she had lost. Suddenly, the thought of escaping to a new place with new people had enormous appeal.

Less than a year after the tragic loss of her husband, son and daughter, Mom started a relationship with a man that she knew nothing about. They only actually met a few times before things took a turn toward the serious. Mom's family and friends were very concerned. Her support system was in Pennsylvania. They pleaded with her not to marry this man that she knew nothing about.

Fourteen months after the car wreck, Mom married this man from Tennessee. The wedding was held at our church and we were her flower girls / brides' maids. She said "I do" to a stranger. Our friends and family stood by in stunned disbelief as Mom agreed to uproot us from everything familiar. Tennessee was so far removed from her world that perhaps she thought she could outrun her grief. What she really married was a poisonous spider that would trap and weave us tightly into his web as the years passed.

chapter 5

1964 - tennessee

I was five years old when my Mother married Charles Meagher. Charles didn't waste anytime uprooting and moving us to the country in Tennessee. He was desperate to get money in order to create his dream ranch. He often preached that the best investment was land, (even if you didn't have a penny to do anything with it.) The easiest way for him to achieve this goal was to marry money. He figured out pretty fast that Mom was financially independent and decided that he was just the man to take that money from her. We packed up all of our belongings along with Tinkerbell, the cat and headed for the hills of Tennessee.

The ranch was called "The Flying M Ranch" because there was land, cattle, horses, airplanes, and lots of dust. It was quite a conglomeration and unsuccessful in each adventure; but more on that later. Charles had big dreams of owning a ranch like those seen in the John Wayne movies.

There is no double that Charles was a very intelligent man. It is said that there is only a thin line between the brilliant and the insane. He was a short, squat and round little man with very little hair and a significant double chin. He had mangled fingers on one hand from a gun accident as a teenager where he inadvertently blew the tips off of his fingers. He had beady little dirt-brown eyes and a nervous habit of always picking at his face so that his cheeks and neck were constantly covered with scabs and bleeding wounds. To sum it up, this man was no Prince Charming.

My first impression of the house in Tennessee was that it was cold, dark, smelly and nasty. In Pennsylvania, our home was clean, inviting and equipped with all the modern conveniences. The house on the hill in Prospect was the complete opposite. It was over 100 years old and it was rumored to have once belonged to the granddaughter of Daniel Boone. The story was that Clara Boone Mason had fallen on hard times when her husband dropped dead of mysterious causes. The rumor was that her missing money was hidden somewhere in the house. Charles was consumed with finding this hidden treasure and would often have dreams and visions about where this cache might be. Not surprising was that the only things we ever found were crumbling plaster and rotting wood. Nothing had been done in the way of home improvements in its first century other than the addition of rudimentary electricity and basic indoor plumbing. When we arrived, the house had a limited supply of water, a septic system that rarely worked, and it had no safe means of heat. It was infested with mice, rats, roaches, and flying squirrels.

I remember standing on the gravel driveway in the early morning as the moving truck came up the hill with all of our belongings. I was holding a puppy in my arms that Charles had promised would be my own special dog. As the truck thundered to a stop at the top of the hill, the puppy wiggled out of my arms and jumped down just in time to be crushed beneath the tires of the big truck. It was a symbolic beginning to our new lives.

The house was situated about halfway way up a hill. From a distance, there was a regal air about it, but close inspection revealed that it was well past its glory years. In the tradition of old plantation homesteads, there was a two story front porch. Exterior doors were left open during the summer to make the most of whatever hot breezes might blow through. Having once been painted white, the color on the house had faded to more of a flakey whitewash than an actual paint job. The rusted tin roof was a constant source of noise with any weather changes. The railings on the porches resembled rotted teeth, while the floor was sawdust waiting to happen. Inside, the faded and stained wallpaper clung to the walls as a testimony to various water leaks over the years. Each room was equipped with a fireplace that was deemed unsafe to use because of the age, condition, and variety of creatures that resided inside of the chimneys.

The house was slammed up against a dirt bank at the back. Thus the only view from the tiny and dusty window in the kitchen was of Tennessee red clay. No sunshine snuck through the dirty glass. The windows in the house were so old that they relied on a rope-pulley system to open. The pulley ropes had frayed away long ago, resulting in much effort being required to open the windows in order to capture any air flow. The kitchen was infested with mice and roaches. When we turned the light on, they would scatter in all directions. As a result, it was imperative to turn the light on before entering the kitchen in order to avoid crunching creatures under foot.

While we each had our own bedroom, privacy was limited. In houses of this vintage, space was not wasted on hallways. Each room was connected to the next by way of a door. Therefore, people were always walking through our bedrooms to get to the next. I spent a lot of time crouched down behind my bed in various states of undress while people wandered through my room.

My bedroom was at the front of the house. It connected to the front hallway and also had a door that opened onto the upper porch. Beth's room was next in line, which meant that her room was a passageway to all the bedrooms. Nancy had the bedroom at the very back of the upstairs in what was referred to as the maid's quarters in days gone by. There was a rickety staircase by her room that led down to the kitchen in the back of the house.

The stained and yellow wallpaper in my room concealed a beehive that lived inside the wall next to the fireplace. When I pressed my ear up to the wall and pounded on it, the buzzing would swell to an angry volume. The distinct and very significant drawback to having a bee hive in the wall of my bedroom was that at least twice a year, the bees would swarm. In the confusion of the swarm, hundreds of them would be in flight in my bedroom. The entire window in my room would be covered with honeybees trying to find their way to freedom. In their frustration of unsuccessful escape into the wild blue yonder, I would often be their victim. Seared into my memory was one night when I got stung seven times just trying to get from my closet to my bed. Once I was finally in my bed, the bees would tunnel their way into my sheets in the middle of the night and I would get stung while trying to sleep. It put a new twist on that old saying about not letting the bedbugs bite...

Our ultra modern furniture, which had fit so well in our Pennsylvania home, was completely out of place in this ancient homestead. Mom had the couch cushions recovered with plastic "fabric" so that it would survive in this harsh new environment. Daddy's handmade tables were placed in the living room. It seemed that Charles had been living a bare existence as there was no furniture there to speak of. Our move basically furnished the entire house, even if it did look too glammed up for a country dump.

There was only one bathroom and it was downstairs. The wood had rotted through near the tub, resulting in a 45 degree slope of the floor towards the tub. Walking into the bathroom required caution, as gravity would cause us to slide down the floor and into the tub. The sink was rusted and barely supported by two weak and wobbly metal legs.

Off to the side of the house, there was a big gully. This became our official trash pile/ dump. Anything and everything went in here. When the pungent smells of decaying waste got too strong, or the pile grew too big, we would set it on fire. Frequently we would look outside to find that the fire had spread to the woods. We would gear up with brooms and shovels and drag a hose out there to subdue the flames. Every once in awhile, discarded spray cans would heat up and explode. Nothing more fun than small unexpected explosions.

Our water source was from a well house situated to the side of the house. The pump was temperamental and even on its best days, did not supply the water that we needed.

The house and the ranch became Mom's money pit. Over the years, she spent tens of thousands of dollars from Dad's life insurance money in an effort to make the house habitable and the ranch profitable.

She was not successful in either endeavor as Charles had a constant need for her ready cash. This house was a project in perpetual decline.

Because there was no heat in the house, one of the first investments Mom made was a fuel oil furnace that was installed under the house. After a few years, this heating unit had a mind of its own which in this household was known as "demon possessed." (Charles would often state that something or someone who had not pleased him was demon possessed. We, as children, were often given this label.) Rarely would the furnace start up without prompting in the mornings. For some reason, it became my responsibility to crawl under the house before breakfast each morning and manually ignite this monster. I would hold my breath, knowing that for sure, this would be the day that the entire thing would blow up and I would literally be toast. There were only three downstairs heating vents from the furnace for the entire house. Electric heaters supplied the only source of warmth for the entire upstairs. In the cold winter mornings, Nancy and I would fight for the primo place by the heat vent in the front living room so that we could dress in some type of comfort. To this day, I cannot stand to be cold.

The next project on Mom's list was to remedy the water situation. There was a cave on the property about a mile from the house that was called Cave Springs. Coming out from this cave was a steady bubbling spring. No matter what season, it was like being in an air conditioned room when we walked into the secluded area by the mouth of the cave. It was always fragrant with the smell of mint, which grew wild along the edge of the spring. The water was the same temperature year-round — almost freezing. People would drive to Cave Springs to fill up jugs of water to take home. Charles blocked off the front entrance to the cave and made a reservoir into which he ran a pipe. This became our source of water for the house. The water was gravity fed through this pipe the entire mile to our house to a pump at the bottom of the hill. Theoretically, the pump would then force the water up the hill to the house. In reality, this system only worked about 50% of the time. During the winter months, the water would freeze, resulting in no water at all. To avoid this disaster, we would have to let the faucets drip all night to keep the water flowing. During the summer, the water level would drop due to heat and drought, resulting in a lack of water pressure. We quickly learned not to take anything for granted in the country.

A new kitchen and the addition of another bathroom upstairs were next on the must-haves list. Mom put her designing skills to work. The new kitchen was built where an old porch had been on the side of the house. Mom also added an extension of a bay window eating area. She spared no expense in putting in all of the modern conveniences she had left behind in Pennsylvania, like a dishwasher, garbage disposal and new stove.

In the bay window area, she chose louvered windows that cranked open. These created a slight problem in the summer months when the tree frogs would climb up on the windows to catch insects in the evenings. When we went to open the windows in the mornings, we were always finding squashed frogs between the panes.

At the end of the kitchen was a mud room which became a community wardrobe. All different sizes of jackets, shoes and boots were stacked here. The only person who had exclusive rights to any piece of outerwear was Charles. Everything else was up for grabs. The goal was to find footwear that wouldn't flop off of our feet too easily and jackets in which we could locate our hands inside the sleeves.

The new bathroom was perched on the roof outside of Beth's bedroom. Because of the slope of the roof, the edge of the tub ended up being only about 4 inches off the floor. Mom and Charles called this a sunken tub to make the design flaw seem more exotic. Access to this bathroom was only from Beth's bedroom.

Mom also bought a single bedroom trailer and semi-permanently parked it at the side of the house. This was her solution to a guest room and in all honesty, it was much nicer than staying in the house. It was hooked up with electricity and plumbing and was like a full-sized playhouse as far as we kids were concerned. We would play out these great scenarios pretending that someone was trying to break into the trailer.

While playing in the trailer one day, I got the bright idea that the best way to keep the "bad guys" out was to simply lock the door. I proceeded to do so and gave the door a good slam to make sure it was closed real tight. In my eagerness, I shut my thumb in the door which was now locked tight. It seemed like it took hours for my sisters to get the door open. As soon as I released from the door-trap, I took off running, screaming at the top of my lungs, and leaving a trail of blood in my wake. I made two complete circuits through the house before they were able to tackle me and access the damage. Thankfully the tip was not severed, but the nail was definitely a goner.

The first time we met Charles' three kids, we had a standoff in my bedroom. The Gilliland girls sat on one twin bed, while the Meagher kids perched on the other one. We were sizing each other up, trying to figure out how this was all going to work. There was Victoria, who was three years older than Beth; Charlene, who was Nancy's age, and Daniel, who was about 2 years older than me. According to the divorce agreement, Charles had visitation with his kids on Saturdays. We didn't spend much time with Victoria because she was almost at the age of emancipation. Charlene and Daniel would come regularly for the next few years. Charles didn't actually spend time with his kids when they did come. Mom picked them up and took them home on Saturdays. In the early years, she tried to plan activities for us to do, like sewing projects and games. All of us girls learned to sew early in life on Mom's ancient Singer zigzag sewing machine. We made clothes for Barbie, doll clothes and items for us to wear as well.

Nancy and Charlene bonded quickly with their love for animals and dreams of becoming veterinarians. Daniel was the odd one out, being the only male in the group. He loved hunting and guns, of which we girls had no interests whatsoever.

As we began our life in Tennessee, Mom tried really hard to make everything work. She attempted to make a 100+ year old cinder pile into a livable home. She wanted to believe that we were a happy, blended family. The reality was not so pretty. The house was a firetrap and there was no way that the six of us kids were ever going to "blend."

Our introduction to Tennessee was much like entering a Twilight Zone episode. Things appeared somewhat normal at first, but time would prove them to be very different from our first impressions.

The ranch was hidden in the hills and hollows of Giles County, Tennessee. It was linked to the community via a tiny bridge that Charles had built across a creek. This crossing was barely wide enough for a car to traverse. We would often get gully washers that would turn the placid stream into a raging river, which surged over the top of the bridge. We became quite fearless about driving through the swirling waters while guessing where the edges of safety were. From here, the gutted gravel drive wound its way through some trees to a railroad track that dissected the ranch down the middle. This was the grand entrance to the ranch that was barricaded by a metal gate.

The entire population of the county was so small that the county newspaper only came out once a week. It had all the components of a quaint southern town, along with an active gossip line and a steep social ladder. For us, from a big Yankee city, this was like stepping back 100 years in time. The social shock was overwhelming. We were surrounded by people who said "Y'all" and spoke in slow southern drawls.

There were some early communication snafus. When Mom invited people for dinner, they showed up at noon instead of six in the evening. We then realized that in the south, lunch was referred to as dinner, and dinner was called supper. The land of Dixie moved at a much slower pace of life and our neighbors were still fighting a war whose outcome had been determined one hundred years earlier.

There were a total of three businesses in the metropolis of Prospect. At the top of the hill, there was a mom-and-pop grocery store that featured two gas pumps and the required front porch. We shopped here for basic groceries and feed for the animals, which was kept in a detached garage at the back of the store. Everyone had a running tab at the store that was paid once a month. It was fascinating as a kid to wander up and down the aisle looking at all the items that were available for purchase. Some of the items looked like they had been there longer than the owners. Across the street from the grocery store was the post office. We could fill up the truck with gas and walk across the street to pick up the mail. This was actually a "new" post office. The one we first used when we moved into town was in an ancient wooden building by the railroad track. The decision to upgrade to a new building was made when a big snake fell through the ceiling into the mail room.

The Methodist church sat on the top of the main hill. Straight across as the crow flies, on the crest of another hill, was the cemetery. Just up the street from the church was the local funeral parlor that was run by a family in the basement of their home. The town was split by the same railroad tracks that halved the ranch. There was a filling station located down the hill and across the railroad tracks. This was where people went for their country food staples; R C colas and Moon Pies. It had general snacks, two gas pumps, a bay for car repairs, and four old men who had a perpetual checker game going on under the shade of an oak tree. The owners lived above the filling station where Miss Sadie also had a part-time beauty salon. Not far away was a semi-grocery store run by two dusty old maid sisters. (I don't mean any disrespect by saying this. This was just the way women were categorized in this locality. You were either married, widowed or an old maid.) The sisters' store was really ancient with a screen door hoping for a breeze in the summer and a pot-bellied stove for heat in the winter. They never seemed to have much business, probably due to the fact that they would not run a tab for people.

Prospect was one of those tight-knit southern communities that knew everything about everyone and routinely sliced up their own. The Yankees were hated and discriminated against almost as much as the blacks, who were kept isolated in their own tiny community. The residents were small in numbers, but there was a strictly structured social food chain. Those at the top of the ladder guarded their places ruthlessly. When we first moved in, Mom made a couple attempts to entertain the way she had in Pennsylvania. Her dinner parties fell flat because the people had never experienced anything as fancy as these affairs and she was a Yankee besides. It was a slap in her face. She was desperately trying to fill in the chasm created when she moved so far away from her friends and family.

This small town was joined to the rest of the world by a single-lane bridge. This meant that when approaching the bridge, we had to look carefully to see if there was anything coming the other way. There was only enough room for one vehicle on the bridge at a time. A game of chicken on this structure would have a grim outcome. Add in fog, heavy rain, ice or a dark night (no streetlights), and crossing this bridge became even more challenging. There was no way to turn around on the bridge and backing up could be pretty tricky. When the river flooded a few times each year, the water would surge over the railings of the bridge and flood the entire plain around it. Once the water receded, traffic would resume as usual without any concern or thought that the flooding may have damaged the structural integrity of the bridge.

There were some interesting people that lived around us and some that would have a phenomenal impact on our lives. One such person was Mary Eden. She was a beautiful ebony color and cleaned for us on Thursdays and Fridays. She didn't drive, so someone had to pick her up and drive her home. Bless her heart; she survived all three of us learning to drive. She always kept a tight hold on the door handle. She was a godly woman who would deliver a sharp rebuke when needed. On Fridays, she baked three pies or three cobblers. Two were left for us, and she took the other one home to her family. She was a constant source of stability in an unstable world. She liked to say that when she finally got to Heaven, she was going to just sit down and rest.

Our closest neighbors lived at the bottom of the hill. They were a family consisting of 4 kids with another one on the way. These kids were as different from my Pennsylvania friends as earthlings to Martians. They spoke funny and they always seemed to be dirty, as there really wasn't any grass growing around their house. Their source of light in the kitchen was a single bulb that hung from a cord in the middle of the room. Water was pumped out of a well pump behind the house and hauled by buckets indoors. Wash was done through a hand washer / wringer on the back of the porch. Their toilet was an outhouse haloed with an overwhelming stench, especially in the hot summer months. Chickens roamed around the yard and food always seemed scarce. The mother of this clan was not much older than Beth and Nancy, and the kids stair-stepped from 5 years old on down. We spent a lot of time playing in the creek and making mud pies. When their dad got home from working at the plant, he would get out of the car, slam the door and tell them to "pick up the junk." That was my cue to head home.

There was another "old maid", Miss Clarabelle, who lived off the main road in a tiny house perched on the side of a hill. (In the south, you address older people by putting a "Miss" in front of their first names, whether they are married or not.) She lived with her brother and her main source of entertainment was listening in on the telephone party line. We bought our fresh eggs from her. The house couldn't have had more than 3 rooms with no indoor plumbing. When we went to get the eggs, she would shoo the chickens off of the kitchen table and counters. She was missing a lot of teeth and dipped snuff.

Because we were back in the hills of Tennessee, there were "hollows" all around us. These were basically one-lane roads that came to a dead-end back in between the hills. Often, the people who lived at the ends of these roads had carefully chosen the location of their homesteads. They didn't want to be around other people or society in general. A perfect example of a southern family tree with no branches was a family that lived at the end of Tunnel hollow. They were all blood relatives and lived under one roof. There seemed to be an endless number of them that would come out to gawk at us when we turned around at the end of the road in front of their home. I guess they didn't see strangers very often. They kept reproducing with no outsiders added into the genetic equation. And the kids didn't seem to ever leave the house, even for school. This family would have kept a swarm of social workers buzzing for years. The hair on the back of my neck would stand up whenever we would pass their home.

We learned early not to just go wandering off into the woods. Moonshine was a thriving industry and trespassers not only weren't welcome, but would most likely just disappear. It was not uncommon to see a member of the community stumbling out of the woods with their paper sacks clutched tightly to their chests and a sappy smile on their faces.

The black community was situated across the main road from our house. It was a gathering of clean and well maintained homes. They took care of what was theirs and each other. White people did not venture into this community; not because of a threat of danger, but because it was not socially acceptable. The blacks had their own church just up the road that was pretty as a postcard. On Sundays, their services would go well into the afternoon, and the music that swelled from that house of God would bring a tear to my eye. These were wonderful, caring people.

Prospect was basically a poor, farming community. There was no other industry in the area. More reliable paychecks required a drive 30 or 40 minutes in either direction. The weather had a huge impact on everyone's day-to-day survival. If the weather did not cooperate, it might take years for the farmers to recover. When we first arrived, there were a lot of cotton fields in the area. It was a visual lesson of life, watching people pick cotton by hand all day in the hot sun. There was not enough money to afford the cotton picking machines. It was hard, relentless and backbreaking work. School was let out for two weeks each fall for "cotton pickin' time" so that the kids could help get the crop in.

Everyone had a garden, and freezing and canning of the bounty was a must for survival. Mom always had a closet full of colorful jars of every vegetable and fruit found in the area. We would pick and process everything from garden crops to the blackberries that grew wild around the farm. When picking wild fruit, we got a crash course in Southern pests including blood suckin' ticks and relentless itching-causing chiggers.

When driving around the ranch or the community, it was common to find a lonely chimney standing at attention in the middle of nowhere. This would be the last tribute to the home that had once thrived there. Either the structures had fallen down from disrepair, or they had burned down. It was a testimony to a dying community.

The closest town of any size was about 30 minutes away. Our exposure to Southern culture happened just before the days of racial unrest and integration. We were thick in the heart of the KKK. There was no hesitation about burning a cross in someone's yard that had crossed those invisible socially acceptable limits. The county court house had separate water fountains and bathrooms for whites and blacks. And the blacks always had to say "Yas Mamme" and Nay Surh". This was quite a shock for young girls who had limited exposure to different races before leaping to the south.

Mom tried to pretend that this new life was normal. Our doctors in Pennsylvania had recommended that we do swimming year-round to help strengthen our limbs and backs after the trauma of the wreck. The problem was that the only indoor pool for us to use was an hour away in Huntsville, Alabama. She would try to make it a fun outing by taking us out to dinner afterwards at a "nice" restaurant. Shoney's was a fancy as it got in Huntsville in the 60's. It was at this restaurant that I fell in love with Captain's wafers and the infamous hot fudge cake. I probably would have swum miles to get those two food items.

We were each trying to cope in our own special ways. We would set up a hospital ward for our baby dolls on the upstairs front porch. It was complete with the mementoes of our hospital experiences including glass IV bottles and tubings. Sadly, we had a high mortality rate among our plastic patients. We also spent hours playing with all of our Barbie gadgets. There was the Barbie Dream house, the Barbie kitchen and the Barbie Fashion show. We would take days to get everything set up just so. Our Barbie and Ken dolls had two sport cars which were always plunging down the front steps of the house, crashing into the antique cabinet by the door. There were rarely any survivors.

Our attempts to blend with our step-siblings were slow at best, but Mom's attempts to make us accept Charles' parents as grandparents never jelled. Charles' widowed mother had married a farmer near Chattanooga, TN. The journey to their home was packed with hairpin turns and twists so severe, that we would be plagued with motion sickness in no time flat. Their farm was comprised of a lot of outbuildings that were in good repair and were actually used for their original purpose. There was a well room that was fed from an underground stream. We would walk down steps to get into it where the entire floor was covered with about 2 feet of ice cold water. The milk cans were stored here, waiting to be picked up by the dairy. However, their house smelled like sickness and pending death. Grandma Umstead had Parkinson's disease and would tremble so badly that she had to be spoon fed by a steadier hand. Mom was puzzled over our reluctance to kiss our new step-grandpa. She finally asked what the issue was and we told her that we didn't like it when he stuck his tongue in our mouths. After that, our interactions with Grandpa Umstead were closely supervised by Mom.

chapter 6

1965

Our first year in Tennessee was quite an adjustment from city life. Everything seemed so much harder in the South. Grocery stores, clothing stores, restaurants and the general conveniences of normal everyday life were not readily available. Then there was the issue of school.

The local schools were small and had not earned high marks in the academic department. Mom was determined that we would get a good education. Her first pick were the schools in Athens, Alabama, about a 30 minute drive away. To complicate matters, we were transferring from Pennsylvania in the middle of the scholastic calendar. Even though I was halfway through the first grade, my October birthday put me past the accepted cutoff for enrollment in Alabama. This necessitated finding an alternative until I started second grade. Her first solution was a brief four day educational stint in Athens. Beth and Nancy were in the public school while I was enrolled in a private

Church of Christ school. Just when we started to settle in, she changed her mind. We ended up in a small school about 20 minutes from home, in a tiny place called Elkmont. The town was centered around two cotton mills which provided jobs for the families in the area. One cotton mill stood at the entrance to the town and the other one marked the exit.

The school was situated on the top of a hill and our carpool left us at the bottom, which meant that we spent a lot of time walking up and down that summit. It was one large building with old wooden floors that were coated with linseed oil. The janitor mechanically moved a huge push-broom up and down the halls all day long. In the tradition of the old South, the cafeteria was detached from the rest of the school and could only be reached by trekking through the weather. There was no air-conditioning, and the windows were kept open to capture any air movement. There wasn't any playground equipment outside; just a barren field where we would run around at recess. Everything in the school was ancient including the books, the plumbing, and the ideas.

In short order, Mom was summoned to the school because the teachers said that we were disrespectful. When she got it all sorted out, the kernel of contention was that we said "yes" and "no" when spoken to, and not the southern requirement of "yes ma'am" and "no sir." We learned right quick to imitate the accent and responses around us in order to survive.

My biggest recollection of my first grade experiences in Elkmont was that I was positively and absolutely terrified of my teacher. Her name was Miss Brack, and she had some type of club foot issue that had never been addressed. As a result, she stomped around on the squashed toe of one shoe and was a very angry woman. She had no qualms about pulling down pants and spanking her students in the front of the entire class. Being a foreigner from the North, I already had a huge target on my back. The civil war was still being fought here, even if it meant on an individual basis. It is a wonder that I slept at all those 5 months of first grade. Miss Brack would write our spelling words on the chalk board at the back of the class. One day I turned around to see the word "elephant." I was terrified that I would never be able to spell this word and would be the recipient of a public spanking and more humiliation. Dreams about first grade can still wake me up in a hot sweat in the dark of the night.

Like all good Prospectians, we attended the Methodist church which rested on crest of the hill on the main street in Prospect. The church was an ancient, crumbling red brick building. Its hidden treasure was the most beautiful stained glass windows only revealed when inside the sanctuary. This was the meeting place for the "society" people of the town. My mother, being a dammed Yankee and all, was never accepted by the good Christians of Prospect. It also probably didn't help that they were well aware of the fact that Charles was as crazy as a loon. The smaller the community, the longer the memory.

Mom was trying to handle being newly married, culture shock and dealing with her new constant companion called grief. As a result, she was not doing much mothering. Nancy and I were pretty much out of control at this point. We started a contest to see who could go the longest without bathing or brushing our teeth. Our downfall was bragging about it in church one Sunday in front of the Prospect society. Mom was mortified and put an end to our pigfest.

One perk to the ranch was the exposure to new and bigger animals. Charles had a Shetland pony named Sputnik. Sputnik did not like to be ridden. His entire goal while we were riding him was to convince us that we did not want to ever do it again. He would jar the teeth out of our heads when he trotted (never galloping or breaking a sweat.) He was also an accomplished bucker. We had to stick to his back like a burr, because he excelled at tossing unprepared riders onto the ground. He would never jump a ditch like the other horses. Instead, he would trot down the pasture at his top speed and then come to a complete stop before crossing the ditch. If we were unprepared for this grinding halt, over his head we topple into the muck.

This new accessibility to horses put a whole new twist on playing cops and robbers. My baby dolls were the frequent victims of brutal kidnappings when they were snatched from the tree house. I would scream in anguish as the kidnappers galloped away while twirling my precious babies over their heads.

There were several barns on the property that we called "Tennessee barns." (This does not in any way imply that any other barns in the state looked like the ones from our childhood, but by that simple term, we have an immediate mental picture of a barn with holes in the roof, half of the wood slats kicked off the sides by horses, a hayloft filled with holes in the floor, and the entire structure surrounded by a wet, cold manure mixture.) Very few of the barns on the Flying M Ranch were functional.

To differentiate the barns, we named them. There was the barn down the pasture and around a corner on the right that was the main feeding barn and where the corral was located. This barn was called "Shoney's barn" as Shoney's was our favorite down-south restaurant. Then there was the Henderson barn which was a mile or so up the road next to a house where a family named Henderson had once lived. A few years later, Charles purchased a farm that was comprised of several hills and had a lake. This was a really pretty place, so it was christened Shangri-La. This barn had an actual manger built into the center of the hayloft. We could toss the hay directly into it to feed the cows and horses during the winter. It was at Shangri-La that we would ride the horses to the lake and take them swimming. They would glide through the water like sea spirits while we hung on to their manes. It was a fun way to get temporary relief from the sweltering heat.

We each had our own special dog, even though there seemed to be an endless supply of them on the ranch. Nancy had a dog name Nosie, who was the sole survivor from his litter when the rest of the pack was killed by a train. He was black with white trim and got his name because he loved to give nose kisses. Nancy would curl up next to him inside his dog house and tell him all of her woes. Apparently, Nosie was also a good listener. Beth had a dog name Kissie. She liked to lick people, which accounts for her very original name. Kissie was kept tied up at the bottom of the hill under an old trailer. Her claim to fame was giving birth to 18 puppies and raising all of them. Honestly, I can't remember the name of my special dog, because over the years, there were so many.

On any given day inside the house, we would have 6 or 7 red wasps flying around in our rooms, or banging around a window. We made little, if any, attempts to spray for bugs, as it was an endless battle. On one particular night, my sisters and I were in our pajamas, and were armed with fly swatters. We were having a high time of going after the wasps. What made it more fun, in a sick and twisted way, was the ever present element of danger. If the wasp got angry enough, and we failed to disable it, then we would get stung. We were having a lively time of it and were dancing around, swatting and screaming when Charles yelled at us to stop. Hearing kids jumping around upstairs would always send him into a tizzy. The wasps were really buzzing by this time, so it was imperative that we finish them off. This pushed Charles into a real rage. He and Mom started through the rooms to deal out our punishment. The unfairness in all of this was that my room was the first room, which meant that I was going to get it while they were still mad and before they got worn out. I ducked under my covers and stayed very still. They became even more enraged because they couldn't find me. (I was pretty small, very skinny and hardly made a dent under the covers.) I then made the fatal mistake of peaking out from under the covers to see where they were. I was on the receiving end of the brunt of their wrath. By the time they finished with me, they were so tired that my sisters got off scott-free.

Even though I was the youngest of the kids, I was not spoiled. This position only meant that I was stuck on the ranch the longest of all the kids. I had to work just as hard as my older siblings and since I was smaller, I had to work faster to keep up. The kaper chart from Pennsylvania had followed us to Tennessee, but instead of 5 slots on the wheel, now there were only three. Our rotational duties were cook, hopper and cleanup. On our week to cook, we were responsible for cooking all of the meals when we were home. The hopper had to set and clear the table, while the cleanup duties meant washing all the dishes, sweeping the kitchen and taking out the trash. There was always something we were supposed to be doing. Mom and Charles always said that I had a bad case of lead bottom. That was their way of saying that I was lazy. I don't ever remember having time to be lazy. It seemed like there was always something that had to be done yesterday. I know that I worked from sunrise to sunset and would tumble into bed exhausted, only to get to repeat it again the next day. Each day on that ranch we walked straight through exhaustion and beyond. I was also told that I was hard headed on a regular basis. I believe the hard headed part. It is probably a result of all the blows to my head.

Another disadvantage to being the youngest of three girls was that I rarely, if ever got something new to wear. I was plagued with the curse of the hand-me-down clothes. For some reason, Mom thought it was just precious to dress the three of us alike. As a result, my wardrobe was very monotonous because I had to wear the same dress three different times, as I grew through the three sizes. I imagine that my teachers were also tired of my déjà vu wardrobe.

Our family car was a very un-cool International Travelall. This was a monster of a station wagon that came in limited ugly colors. Surprisingly, it did have an added AC unit under the dash in the front, but it only blew out a minute leak of cool air when going full blast. Since this vehicle was so unluxurious, it was a mystery as to why Mom felt compelled to cover the seats with plastic seat covers. They had a raised plastic bump pattern on them, so that when we reached our destination and exited from the stifling hot car, any exposed extremities were decorated with a branded imprint from the seat covers. For the most part, our vehicles all had 4/55 air-conditioning. In other words, our cooling was dependent on whatever breeze could be generated when the four widows were cranked all the way down and we reached our cruising speed of 55 miles per hour.

For Christmas that year, we took our first and last family car trip. Mom wanted to spend the holiday with one of her sisters and mother, which meant a two day drive from Tennessee to Denver, Colorado in the Travelall station wagon. Charlene and Daniel went with us, which meant that there were seven of us crammed into the car. Mom and Charles were in the pilot / co-pilot positions up front. Daniel and I shared the second seat, while Beth, Nancy and Charlene set up a bed in the cargo area for the long haul. The only touristy thing of the drive that I remember was a quick and unentertaining stop in Dodge City along the way. I was prone to car sickness and had one episode of explosive emesis into a baggie hastily passed back to me by Mom. The problem was that the baggie was defective and Daniel and I were soon covered in the remains of my most recent meal, with no way to clean up ourselves or clean out the car.

My most vivid memory of the trip was running out of gas on the Interstate a few hours away from our final destination. Charles was adamant about not stopping for gasoline until the car had less than a quarter of a tank registering. He failed to calculate into the equation the distance to a gas station that would actually be open late on the holiday night. This resulted in the seven of us being stranded for hours along the Interstate in the cold of the winter. It is safe to say that no one in the station wagon was happy about our plight and things became very vocal at times. Charles' shouting admonitions to pray were not helpful either. It was hard not to compare this Christmas vacation ordeal with the way things had been not so long ago. A trucker finally stopped to rescue us. He gave Charles a ride to the nearest open gas station, while we waited, shivering in the car. Hands down, this was the worst Christmas of my life.

Other attempts to take some family vacations with our blended family of 8 were equally as memorable. Mix all 6 kids together on an out-of-town adventure and it was a recipe for disaster. Our mode of vacation transportation was now strictly by private plane. We would fly to these destinations crammed like sardines into the small cabin of the aircraft. Because I was the smallest, I would often end up in the baggage compartment, or on the floor underneath everyone's feet. There were some really special memories, like our trip to the World's Fair in New York City. Our family was actually evicted from a NYC hotel. Or the time when Beth got airsick and vomited into Charles' hat. The improvised vomit receptacle was then tossed out of the plane to descend towards an unsuspecting victim down below. Then there was the especially disastrous trip to Florida, where we got booted out of a hotel after knocking on random hotel room doors and peeping through the windows in the bar. Beth also ended up with second degree sunburn. Just too much forced family fun.

chapter 7

1966

By 1966, Mom had us settled in school in Alabama. These schools were more comparable to those we attended in Pennsylvania. For example, the teachers did not actually beat us in front of the entire class. Mom was trying to pretend that we weren't making sacrifices, so we were enrolled in baton twirling classes (a skill that every Southern Belle should know). It was my second grade teacher who moonlighted as the baton teacher, so it made it convenient for those after school lessons. We performed our skills in all of the school and holiday parades. Costumes were not ordered from catalogs, but had to be sewn at home. Mom got pretty adept at making our parade costumes adorned with lots of sequins and fringe. I can still twirl a mean stick, which sadly is a talent that I have not found to be a very valuable commodity in everyday life.

Then there were the piano lessons after school once a week. I had to walk several blocks to my piano teacher's home. This sweet lady had a real soft-spot for me. I don't know why, as I was by no means a star pianist. I rarely practiced and would only do my written piano bookwork in her parlor as I waited for my lesson to begin. On rare occasions, she would treat me to a Coca-Cola on a hot afternoon. She had the little glass bottles of Coke that she would put in her freezer just long enough for them to get icy. It was like heaven in a bottle.

I continued to be an extrovert, thinking that a career in entertainment would bring much joy to the world. After seeing the Sound of Music in the movie theater, I was mesmerized by the songs and dancing. We bought the record with the sound track and I would practice every night creating dances to go along with my lip-synching performances. When I had my routines down perfectly, I would perform these for show- and-tell at school. I was convinced that everyone loved my dances and could hardly wait for the next show-and-tell to present a new rendition for my third grade class.

Within months of his marriage to our mom, Charles quit his job in Huntsville so that he could devote his time to creating the ranch he had always dreamed of. He hung up his suits and ties forever. His new work uniforms for the Flying M Ranch consisted of dark blue Dickies with a belt that he would wear day-in and day-out. He wore these around the ranch, to town, to church, and all the places in between.

Charles was the master manipulator. With our Dad's life insurance money and the monthly social security checks, he now had the piggy bank to begin building his dream. Our monthly social security checks insured that he didn't have to spend a dime on us. He was in high cotton and was enjoying this new financial windfall. He spent the majority of his time sitting at the head of the table drinking huge glasses of sweet tea. We would make gallons each day for his unrelenting thirst. He would guzzle it down in a few swallows while he pondered the problems of the day.

Charles had a few cows but decided that he needed to spend big bucks on a registered bull in order to build a quality herd. The purchased bull was named Vindicator, after a bull in a John Wayne movie. (There's that Hollywood dream again.) He was a big burly guy that bred calves so large that many of our cows couldn't birth them. The cattle herd never seemed to be the gold mine that Charles had envisioned. Even with the "input" from this prize bull, the cattle sales rarely brought a profit.

Charles also had visions of making it rich in the horse business. We had some basic saddle horses, but he dreamed of having a real "gen-u-wine" horse farm. He began purchasing registered Tennessee Walking Horses, with plans to breed them and sell the colts for profit. Along with the horses came the other must-haves, such as the fancy bridles, saddles, saddle blankets, and even a horse trailer. In the beginning, Beth and Nancy even competed in some horse shows.

This fantasy was short lived however. With no management, planning and supervision, the horses began inbreeding. This polluted the registered lines. It was anyone's guess as to who the sire of the colts might be. Without consistent handling and training, they became wild and out of control.

One day, a mare gave birth close to the house. Charles tied the new momma to a tree in the front yard so that he could carry the colt into the house for everyone to see. When we came back out of the house, the mare had literally dropped dead in the front yard, still tied to the tree. We were now the surrogate parents to a brand new colt. Mom named the little filly Flicka. She had a chestnut coat with a white blaze down her nose and four white stockings. Miraculously, Flicka survived and then thrived. She was soon chasing us down to get her bottle. Colts grow by leaps and bounds, and she quickly moved from a cute little filly to a big hairy monster. She took sadistic delight in stepping on our toes and smashing us up against the fence. It took careful planning and cunning to sneak out of the squeaky back door with her bottle, climb up the hill to the pasture behind the house and slide the bottle into the holder without her hearing or seeing us. Since it was a matter of survival, it was imperative to be invisible. Not only would she prance on our feet, but she would pivot while on top of our feet to make sure that we felt it. Flicka was just one of the many diversified personalities that made up our horse family.

In the horse mix, we had a black stallion that Charles named Domino. Nancy and I called him "Doo-Doo Head" which was a much more appropriate name. He was the product of inbreeding and no training. Doo-Doo Head believed that he was the king of the horses and would fight to prove his point. He was kept separate from the mares that were saddle broken, and his one mission in life was to have all of the mares on the ranch together in his pasture. It was impossible to predict where he might be at any given time, and if it would be safe to ride across the field. One day while I was riding one of the mares, he appeared like a tornado from nowhere. He began rearing up and pawing at me with his hooves. He smashed my hand on the saddle horn where I was clinging for dear life. I was finally able to slide out of the saddle on the other side and race to the fence for safety. I vaulted over the fence onto the railroad track in the nick of time as he thundered up for the kill. I really did hate that horse.

Only two other horses are worth remembering. One was a chestnut mare named Robinson. She was a really good saddle horse and great to ride during round-ups. Unfortunately, Charles would always ride her because she was the best. It was entertaining to watch her brace herself and lock her legs when he was trying to climb up into the saddle. Too bad that we couldn't hear what she was telling the other horses about having to carry all of that weight around for the long day.

The second horse was named Blondie. She was a palomino and was a gentle ride. The only problem with Blondie was that she did not like to be left behind. She was what we called a follower. As long as Robinson was in front, we didn't really even have to hold onto the reins, as Blondie would go in the path of Robinson's hooves. Blondie did have a nasty habit during round-up time of trying to scrap her rider off by brushing up against every tree along the way. It got very annoying and painful.

If we were riding the horses and heard the lonely whistle of an approaching train, we would get into position. As soon as the train was even with us, we would take off galloping down the pasture, racing the train to the finish. It was even more fun if it was a passenger train. We would keep up the chase until the caboose had passed on by. The race did require vigilance and care as there were a lot of hidden ground hog holes in the pasture that could lame a horse during our flight down the field.

One time, Charles and I were trying to round up some stray cows that had wondered onto another farmer's property. Charles was in front riding Robinson, and I was in back, of course, on Blondie. We had mounted up in a clearing, and in the process, I had lost my hat. Hats were important because they kept our long hair up and out of the way. While Charles took off on Robinson through the trees, I had to dismount to get my hat. Blondie was in a panic by the time I was barely settled back in the saddle. She took off like a rocket, because she couldn't see Robinson anymore. She dashed under a low lying limb, and the last thing I remember was seeing her blond tail as I somersaulted off of her back and landed on the ground, getting knocked out. Some time passed before I regained consciousness and was able to pick myself up off of the ground. I had a bloody nose and taking a deep breath was like a hot poker in my side. I was wandering around trying to find my runaway horse, holding my cracked ribs when I finally spotted Charles meandering around the pasture. Blondie, the traitor, was over by the pond taking deep drinks of the water. Charles deemed that I was fit and directed me to ride Robinson home through the woods, leading Blondie behind. So goes that old saying about when you fall off the horse, you have to get back in the saddle, damaged ribs, concussion and all.

Another one of Charles's impulsive purchases was a herd of goats. He decided that the goats would be our answer to weed control. He concluded that they would eat up the overgrowth, which would cut down on the required bush-hogging. He chose a herd of stiff-legged goats. What this meant was that when the goats got startled, their legs would literally lock on them and they would fall over. Theoretically, they were easier to keep contained or fenced in. However, it quickly became apparent that the stiff-legged feature on the Flying M Ranch would be a fatal genetic flaw. The theory about Survival of the Fittest came into play in very real way. When a dog or other critter got hungry, all they had to do was to run up the goats and startle them. Immediately, the goats would be petrified with fear and topple over onto their sides, which made for easy pickins'.

The train was another danger area for the goats. The railroad track literally dissected the ranch. The fences along the train track were barely upright, supported only by brush and briars, because the actual fence posts had rotted out years ago. The overgrowth was more of a fence line than the actual existence of wooden posts and wire. On one memorable night, the entire herd of goats was wandering along the tracks when the train came along blowing its whistle. The noise startled the goats, resulting in the locking of their legs, and a predictable end to this story. The train wiped out about two-thirds of the herd. We became surrogate mothers to four kids whose mothers were killed by the train. The three of us took turns getting up every couple of hours for the next few weeks to feed the babies in the laundry-turned-nursery.

At Christmas that year, we were thick into the goat business. I had reached the age when I began to question the existence of Santa Clause. Mom concocted a plan to renew my belief in Santa that would utilize the always available goat poop. To my delight on Christmas morning, I found "Reindeer poop" on the carpet in the house. Rest assured, I was the only kid who went back to school proclaiming that Rudolf had pooped in her house.

Forgetfulness was also another flaw of the goats. The mothers would conceal their babies in the undergrowth while they went off to graze and forget where they left them. Or they would hide their kids whenever danger was near to protect them, and the nannies would be killed. Being a goat was a hard life, but being a goat kid was even harder. One of our special "kids" was named Nanny. Nanny's mother had hidden her in a clump of grass and never came back to get her. By the time we found Nanny, she was scared and starving. We raised her on the bottle and she was as much a family pet as the dogs and cats were. The problem was that Nanny truly believed in her heart that she was a dog. Surprisingly, the dogs accepted her as one of their own and didn't try to harm her in any way. Being country dogs, our dogs would chase any cars that came up the hill and bite the tires. It was pretty comical to see this goat running along with the dog pack, "baa-hing" at the car and putting her mouth on the tires. One time the dogs took off hunting and Nanny went along with them. When the dogs came back, there was no Nanny. We frantically tried to find her. Finally, after about 10 days, we got a call from a poor family back in one of the hollows. Nanny was at their house and it had taken several days for them to figure out whom she belonged to. It was a miracle they didn't eat her, as free goat would feed a family for several days. They knew right away that Nanny was someone's special pet because she came inside and made herself right at home.

One day Mom brought Nanny to my elementary school for show-and-tell. I had entertained the kids with all kinds of stories about my beloved pet. I am sure they had doubts that any goat could be so marvelous. But Nanny won them over in no time at all. Her days were numbered, however. She had a bad habit of sleeping with her head tucked behind the tire on the car. One afternoon, Mom hopped in the car in a hurry and backed-up. And that was the end of Nanny.

There wasn't much time for play on the ranch. (Of course, there was more time in the beginning when Charles actually had a job.) One of the things that we did do for fun in those early days was to play in the creek that ran through the front pasture. In the summer, we would wade in it, trying to stay upright on the smooth rocks in the water that were coated with green algae. In some areas, the rocks would have little black periwinkles clinging to them, which would give a little traction when we rock-skated. The creek was filled with crawdads and minnows, along with various poisonous snakes. Did I mention that I am terrified of snakes?

My stepbrother was obsessed with snakes. He would spend his entire Saturdays out in the woods hunting. He liked to bring back the snakes that he had killed and use them to scare us. I remember one time hearing a knock on the front door. When I went to answer it, Daniel was hiding around the corner and had wrapped a dead snake around the door knob that I now had my hand on. Yuck!

When the rains came, the creek would swell up and overflow its banks. We still had the remnants of Raymond's Styrofoam sailboat from Pennsylvania. Over time, it had broken into three segments. We played with these three pieces of Styrofoam for years. We would climb onto the boat chunks and fly down the flooded creek. We had no worries about the dangers involved in this endeavor, such as death, drowning or tangling up in the barbed-wire fence gaps. These were floating fences that were strung across the creek to keep the cows from straying off onto the next farmer's land. The trick was to get to the creek bank before we got caught in the sharp wire and then trudge around the barrier. One time, I fell off of my "boat" and got trapped up under a root of a tree along the creek bed. The water was too swift for me to be able to pull myself out and the roar of the flood was too loud for anyone to hear my cries for help. I was afraid to let go, as I had no idea if I would float on through or get tangled up in the roots and drown. Finally, one of the bigger kids came by and pulled me out. This near tragedy didn't damper our thirst for white water adventures at all.

During another of our creek episodes, two of us were sharing the same small piece of Styrofoam. When we rounded a bend, we got tangled up in a tree and some vines. Imagine my surprise to see a snake coiled around one of the branches right by the head of my boat mate. In my panic, I jumped off of the boat into the raging torrent just as the snake uncurled and dropped into the water. That might have been the closest anyone has come to walking on water since the real deal.

It was also a daring adventure to take turns going through the culvert that was underneath our home bridge. This was a bit risky because if the water was running fast, debris and junk would wash up inside and get clogged up. Add an average sized kid and it would pack the obstruction a little tighter. When there was a good flood going on, there would actually be a whirlpool on the upper side, which would suck objects in faster than we could feed them. We could always count on the creek for new diversions and entertainment.

A few times we went spelunking in Cave Springs, the place where we got our water for the house. We would do this without any adult supervision. The entrance to the cave had a very small diameter, which meant that we had to crawl on our bellies for several feet in ice-cold water. It was so cold inside the cave, that I would turn blue the minute I wiggled inside. It was amazing to experience absolute darkness. We would crawl around on our hands and knees exploring the different "rooms" in the cave. We had names for them based on the unique features they had. There was one room that had a rounded floor with lines of ripples in it. We called this the cabbage room, because it was as if we were sitting on top of a big head of cabbage. There were tons of stalactites and stalagmites in all colors, shapes and sizes. It was always a race to see if our flashlight batteries would last until we got out of the cave. At the back of the cave, there was a huge pile of rocks from an earlier cave-in.   Without a doubt, we worked our guardian angels overtime.

Occasionally, we would have snow during the winter. Having lived in the north, we had the best variety of sleds in the county. In addition, living on a hill made us the prime sledding location. We would hop on the sleds at the top of the hill and fly down at incredible speeds. As we neared the bottom, it took some real skill to either turn the sled 90 degrees or roll off before hitting the fence at the bottom of the hill.

Cow patty fights were another source of entertainment. In the country, everything that is green is not grass. This was one contest in which no one wanted to be the loser. The trick was to pick up a cow patty that was dry on the top, but was still wet on the underside. We would throw this with all of our might at the head of our opponent. With any luck, the cow patty would do a perfect turn in the air, smacking our target with the wet side down. There is nothing like a little cow manure to put a pleasant odor in the day.

chapter 8

1967

We soon left the Methodist Church in Prospect for a larger Baptist church in Alabama. The miracle about this change was that this church was led by a truly awesome man who really loved the Lord. His name was Brother Jennings. It was in this church that my sisters and I would hear the true word of God and come to have a personal relationship with Him. A lot of the kids from our schools also attended, which made the whole church experience much more enjoyable.

Charles now decided to start an airplane repair business. He and Mom were both aeronautical engineers and pilots. We (and I literally mean we) built a hangar at the bottom of the hill for this new business and we began buying and repairing airplanes. The new business was named Jonathan's Flying Service.

The hanger was a nightmare of what any normal person would call junk. Charles was the ultimate hoarder. There were parts stacked several feet high with only a small walking path in between. We were often sent down to the hanger on a scavenger hunt to find a small part or a tool. I spent hours walking around those piles of junk trying to find the needle in the haystack. We were forbidden to return to the house until we found the specific item. I remember being down there in the airplane graveyard for so long that they actually forgot that I was still down there looking for the object. Sometimes I just gave up, sat down on a box and had a good ol' cry.

We would help build airplane engines, overhaul engines, and strip, recover and paint the planes. At any given time, we would have 3 or 4 small planes tied up around the ranch. There was a large flat pasture at the bottom of the hill that became the official "runway". A windsock was erected along the railroad track and a gas tank was installed near the airplane hanger. It took an experienced pilot to take off from the runway with a ditch at one end of the field and a gas tank and hill at the other end. It took an *expert* pilot to be able to successfully land a plane on this makeshift runway, with the aforementioned obstacles plus grazing cows to be dodged. The ultimate goal was to not run out of grass during the landing and to not pick up any bovine baggage along the way.

We spent hours working on the planes. The fabric had to be ripped off and then the fuselage had to be sanded and repaired for the new fabric. Many of the planes we worked on were crop dusters, so the fabric was saturated with dangerous chemicals used to kill pests. There was no concern or precautions taken about the health hazards this chemical exposure might pose. Once stripped, the wings would be placed on saw horses while the new fabric was applied. The fabric had to be glued on with a substance that we called "dope." If enough was inhaled, we would feel pretty fuzzy. When the "dope" dried on our hands, it made a second skin that would crack and curl up. Hours were spent each night pulling it off with our teeth while we finished up our other chores.

After the fabric was applied, the fabric joints had to be sanded by hand. If we sanded too hard, it would result in a hole in the fabric, which was not a good thing. If we didn't sand hard enough, then the paint would not have a smooth finish. This process would take weeks to complete.

Next, the wings were suspended from the ceiling by wires for painting. Charles would decide what kind of design or stripes would be on the plane and these areas had to be masked off with masking tape and paper as each individual color was sprayed. This was the tricky part. If the tape wasn't pressed down securely, then it would result in over-spray that had to be rubbed off by hand. If the tape was too sticky, got too hot or was left on too long, then the adhesive would literally tear chunks of paint off when removed and we would be on the doo-doo list for many days. The ultimate goal was to not be around when the tape had to be removed to avoid getting blamed. I can't even estimate how many stripes and airplane numbers we masked off over the years.

Finally we were ready to face the nightmare of reassembling all the pieces to finish with a (hopefully) complete airplane. The worst part was standing for what seemed like hours with our hands up over our heads, literally holding up the airplane wings. The wings had to be held perfectly still while Charles would take his sweet time lining up the bolt holes with the struts to reattach them to the plane. There were no allowances or breaks for cramping muscles. It didn't help that I was the shortest in the bunch and could only reach the wings by standing on my tippy toes. We also did repair work on gliders and helicopters. The basic rule was that if a pilot could land it on the Flying M Ranch or drag it in, then we would repair it.

As the smallest in the family, I inherited the jobs that involved tight, tiny and restrictive spaces. When we were rebuilding a metal plane, my job was to crawl into the very front of the plane into a confined space so small that once I was in there, I couldn't turn around. I then had to direct the person on the outside so that the pieces could be riveted together. I was also the designated flashlight holder. This meant holding the flashlight so that the area being worked on was totally illuminated, with zero wavering. The job might last for hours. If my arm wearied, that was just too bad. The light still had to be kept still and focused to avoid undesirable consequences.

Around this time Mom and Charles decided to open an airstrip in Athens, Alabama where we went to school and church. The airstrip consisted of a single wide trailer, which functioned as the office and a home-away-from-home, a flat strip of land between two cotton fields, and a gasoline tank. It was on a graveled lot that was shared with an abandoned concrete plant next door. I was never sure what kind of items they had made there, but the entire area was surrounded by mounds of sand. As kids, we would spend hours inside the metal building exploring the equipment that was petrified with dried concrete.

At the airport we were kept busy logging planes in and out, filling them up with gas, and my personal assignment - retrieving the tow-rope used for the gliders. There seemed to be an endless supply of people who wanted to take flying lessons. The tradition was that when someone soloed in a plane, a piece of fabric was cut off from the back of their shirt. Their name and the date of this accomplishment were then written on the shirt scrap and it was stapled to the ceiling of the office trailer. When people looked up at the ceiling, they could see a whole story of flying accomplishments.

Along with learning how to fly, we offered airplane rides, glider rides and the opportunity to solo in the glider. The tow plane would be attached to the glider by a long rope that had a metal ring on each end. As the plane would take off down the field, the rope would get tight and the glider would be towed along behind it. Best case scenario was that the plane and glider would pick up enough speed so that they would both be airborne by the time they were out of grass and into the power lines. When the glider reached the desired altitude, the tow rope would be released from the glider. The plane would then circle the airport after releasing the glider and drop the tow rope onto the field, and then land. I had to watch carefully to see where the rope fell, or it would require much hunting to locate it in the cotton field. The airport in Athens consumed our afternoons, weekends, and summers.

Mom was still a good sport about letting us keep critters for pets. I went through a hamster phase and progressed into the gerbil business in a big way. I had two cages of gerbils at one point and they were reproducing so quickly, that I had an arrangement with the owner of a pet store in Athens to buy the babies from me. The cages I had were really deluxe. They were metal on three sides with a full plane of glass on the front and a built in water bottle and exercise wheel. Pretty nice digs for something a few steps above a mouse in the genetic tree. One day, I got an inspirational idea and decided to give my gerbils some fresh air. I think my gerbil census was about 10 or 11 between the parents and the babies. I set the cages out on a table on the top porch outside my bedroom, and went on about my day. When I went to move them back inside later in the evening, I had a nasty surprise. Apparently when the sun started to set, the rays bounced off of the porch railing and projected directly onto the metal cages, cooking my entire Gerbil population. And just like that – I was out of the Gerbil business.

When Mom and Charles first got married, Grandma Jones would come to visit a couple of times a year. She always slept in my room on a twin bed. Even though she snored like a freight train all night long, I felt special to have extra time with her. Grandma Jones was an awesome woman. She had a great sense of humor and didn't take crap off of people. Yet, she was a lady through and through. Charles initially tried to sweet talk her into investing in Tennessee land and airplanes. She rejected him without hesitation. Grandma had no illusions as to what kind of man Charles Meagher was and he hated her because of her insight. After this rebuff, he did everything that he could to hurt and anger her. He called her a man-hater and she turned it right back around on him. She was one of the few people I ever saw that would stand up to him. Of course, this put Mom in the middle of their heated battles. One time when Grandma came to visit, Charles got her so upset that she started having chest pains. That marked the end of her visits to Tennessee, so she instead paid for us to fly out west to visit her in Colorado. She was the one person that might have been able to convince Mom to leave Charles, but Mom would never admit that she had made a phenomenal mistake in marrying this man.

Over the years, Beth maintained her close friendship with our cousin, Donna Sue. Every summer they would spend two weeks together. Donna Sue would fly to Tennessee for a week of a crazy country experience and then they would both fly to Kentucky where Beth would have seven days of what normal life could be like. Donna Sue was our last connection with our relatives from Michigan and those long-ago family reunions. Mom worried about Donna Sue getting a realistic impression about our life in Tennessee, so during the week that she was at our home, Charles was on his best behavior.

The year that Beth and Donna Sue were both 14, it was time for their departure to Kentucky. Mom and Charles flew them to the big airport in Nashville and dropped them off. They didn't go into the terminal with them, but turned the plane around and took back off for Prospect. When the girls went to check in for their flight, it was to find out that their tickets were for a flight the day before. There was no one they could call. Mom and Charles were flying back home and Donna Sue's parents were on their way to the airport in Kentucky to pick them up. Thankfully the person at the passenger check-in had mercy on them, got them on the next flight to Kentucky and even put them in first class.

chapter 9

1968

Charles was a scary man and became more rabid with power as the years passed. He was also a religious fanatic. He intimidated, terrorized, punished and used his god as a weapon to control those around him. Every morning began with breakfast, then reading a chapter in the Bible, followed by a long repetitious prayer. This is pretty much how I learned to read. If a first grader can learn to pronounce the names in the Old Testament, then Jane, Dick and Spot were really no challenge at all. It didn't matter if we were late for school or sick; the Bible was read without fail. We would begin in Genesis and work our way, chapter by chapter, to Revelations. Each chapter was divided into thirds. (I also learned to do fractions early on, to make sure I wasn't getting gypped.) Beth would read her verses, followed by Nancy, and then me. Charles would then pray for about 30 minutes. He would pray for the same people in the same order every day. Some of the people he prayed for had been dead for years, but he still prayed for them. It was more of a chanting than talking to God. He would weave his way through the family tree and then work through everyone in the entire community before he was finished. I would often sneak in a catnap during this monolog, but it was imperative to wakeup before he finished. There were even a couple of times when *he* actually fell asleep while praying. We would jerk awake to his snoring, and realize that we were really going to be late for school.

We were doing well in our schools in Alabama, but our carpools were starting to fizzle out. We had been riding with some neighbors who worked at the schools in Athens, but scheduling conflicts were making the 30 mile trips to and from school difficult. Now that there was access to a rudimentary runway in Alabama, the school transportation problem was solved. Charles would fly us in a plane to our airport in Athens each morning and then fly us home each night. The problem of getting from the airport to the schools was solved with the purchase of an old meter maid cart. Even though Beth was too young to get her driver's license, she was old enough to get her motorcycle license. The meter maid cart consisted of three wheels with a box on the back. That summer, we put our painting skills to work using bright blue and white paint in a cool design. It looked pretty good so far as meter maid carts went. Nancy and I rode inside the box on the back where there was no ventilation. It was hot as an oven in the summer and cold as an ice box in the winter. But at least we were semi-protected from the elements, unlike Beth. She had only two flimsy plastic curtain-things to seal herself in, which never worked in real life. Beth hated the humiliation of driving this freaky thing to school each day. It had a dependable tendency to stall out in high traffic areas. She also resented having to wear a motorcycle helmet because it squashed her hair. Once a motorcycle helmet was pushed down on top of big hair, that hairstyle was not going to ever be the same.

We had many adventures in the meter-maid cart. We were real a dog magnet. They would hear us coming a couple of blocks away and would get ready to pounce. When we came up the street, they would launch themselves into the front of the cart, trying to bite Beth. Nancy and I would be ready in the back with loaded syringes. It only took a couple of squirts until the dogs decided to leave us alone, but there were always new dogs for us to train.

The principal at my elementary school once told my mother that he loved to hear my tardy excuses, because they were always very unique. They often involved airplane problems or other unique things such as cows unwilling to move off of the runway so the plane could take off, snow on the wings that had to be cleared before takeoff or a stalled- out meter maid cart. We were definitely the "freaky" kids at school.

Poor Beth was the substitute mother, having to handle all kinds of emergencies because Mom was 30 miles away in Tennessee. One time, she had to take a cab to my school to pick me up and take me to the doctor to get stitches in my chin after a fall on the playground. Bless her heart, she passed flat out while the doctor was sewing me up and earned a stay on the stretcher beside me.

My extracurricular activities now included dance lessons. Initially, I could walk to the dance studio which was a few blocks from my elementary school. I started with ballet and then added tap and jazz lessons to my repertoire over the next few years. I was only a mediocre dancer, but I did enjoy the classes. I have some really fabulous pictures of me in all of my dance paraphernalia, looking quite ballerina-ish.

At this point, all three of us were in braces. The orthodontist was the only game in town and his office was about 3 blocks from the elementary school; an easy walk after school for my appointments. I was one of those kids that REALLY needed braces. I had the whole buck-tooth thing going and had way too many teeth for my mouth. Before they even started my braces, I had to have 8 teeth pulled. The bad thing about our orthodontist was that he was a smoker and a drinker. Perhaps he needed the fortitude of a hit from the bottle and the nicotine to calm his nerves before he could face his elementary-aged patients in the afternoons. All I remember is that he smelled like an ash tray inside of a distillery.

We had those pre-historic braces that consisted of a main wire that encircled the teeth and attached to bands cemented to the back molars. The orthodontist would then thread individual wires around each tooth and twist, twist, and twist some more until it felt like he was ripping the teeth right out of my head. The pain was intense, both during and after the procedure. I grew to hate this sadistic man as much as he grew to hate me. One day, Beth was in the waiting room waiting for her appointment. All she could hear was some kid in the back exam room crying and screaming their head off. Imagine her embarrassment when I walked out of the exam room with tear tracks down my cheeks. I did eventually reach an understanding with this cruel man. During one exam, I bit his finger. He promptly took my braces off and didn't give me a follow-up appointment. I think we know who won that battle.

Charles loved to quote scripture. He prided himself on his ability to proclaim the perfect scripture for any occasion. He could rattle off any number of verses from the top of his head, especially during an argument. Of course, if we actually took the time to look up the quoted verse, it would reveal that he was not completely accurate. He also loved to take scripture out of context. Scripture versus are a lot like statistics. A person can twist them to backup whatever point they want, by taking them out of context and being selective in the ones they use.

We were living in a cult, and Charles was the leader. He never failed to dish out his daily doses of verbal abuse. He didn't tolerate back talk or sassing of any kind. Rule by rule, he began to try to control every area of our lives. We were not allowed to cut our hair. Long hair, of course, would get in the way of our work, and could also be a hazard, so we had to be very ingenious with ways to keep it up and out of the way. We would pin it to the top of our heads and then get creative in our choice of things to cover our hair. There were old hats that we might find lying around or there was the Aunt Jemimah look. This involved taking a bandana, and through some innovative folding and tying, our hair would be completely covered. Quite a fashion statement.

Another major issue was how we dressed. When Beth was in high school, mini skirts were all the rage. There were many battles over the length of our dresses and skirts. Charles wanted our skirts and dresses to be at the bend of our knee; absolutely no shorter and longer was better. We had to make most of our clothes because anything that met his requirements was definitely out of fashion, which eliminated the store bought items. There was one instance where Charles told Beth to let down the hems of her skirt until they were at her knee. Beth made some helpful suggestions to which Charles took offense. He stormed up the steps. I will never forget the banging, screaming and yelling that we could hear as we huddled downstairs. When it was over, Beth had a bloody nose and Mom never said a word in protest. Beth became very ingenious with some easy fashion tricks that helped her survive. Rolling the waistband of a skirt just a few turns made it a more fashionable length; adding a belt to a dress after leaving the house, and the hem was suddenly shorter by a couple of inches.

Our living situation was deteriorating quickly. On day, in desperation, Beth snuck upstairs and made a long distance call to our church in Athens. She was going to tell them about the abuse and to plead for help. However, as soon as someone answered, she freaked out and hung up the phone. She was afraid of what Charles would do to all of us when he found out. As for all of the other adults in the community around us; not one of them ever tried to help us or protect us from this crazy man.

To this day, I still have gate issues. Wherever we went on the farm there were always gates that had to be unlocked, opened and closed, and re-locked. This was a big pain in the butt as a kid, because we were the ones that always got to be the designated gate openers. The gates never swung open easily, but always seemed to drag on one side. It took all of my strength to lift the drooping end up in order to be able to get it completely open. The front gate at the house always had to be locked at night to keep the visitors out (or the residents in). Charles had a huge key ring that had about 50 keys on it. Most of them probably didn't open anything left on the farm. It took forever to search through all of the keys on the ring to find the "right" key. We never were issued our own set of keys, but had to go to him and ask for the keys in order to do his bidding. Rain, sleet or dark of night always made it more challenging. It was a struggle to find the chain with the lock on it in the dark, while trying to avoid the poison ivy growing up the pole and the creepy crawlies in the overgrowth. The one thing that gave Charles unlimited joy was to wait until the gate opener was concentrating on fitting the key into the rusted lock caught in a tangle of vines and weeds in the pitch black night. When his victim was fully focused on the task at hand, Charles would lay on the horn to see if he could scare the bejesus out of them. The more reaction he got, the harder he laughed. Predictably, after we all moved on in life, they no longer closed the gate, day or night. Perhaps he didn't care if the cows got out, or maybe it was because the residents he had tried to trap, had already escaped.

There was always an endless supply of guns and ammunition around the house. Charles was a firm believer in the right to bear arms and he kept a full arsenal of weapons at his disposal. Target practice was done on a continuous basis, due to the endless supply of varmints. There were ground hogs down on the runway, snakes around the house, and an unlimited variety of unwanted invaders. We were each given our own rifle for Christmas.

One of my favorite gun memories was one night when the dogs started really making a ruckus. Charles was convinced that someone was sneaking around the airplanes trying to steal gasoline. The remedy for this was to fire a few rounds from a pistol into the sky. On this particular night, there was a truck load of cows at the house waiting to go to the cattle auction the next day. Mom went outside and fired off a few rounds into the air. Imagine her surprise to find a dead cow among the sale stock on the truck the next morning – the victim of a falling bullet.

Charles had a hive of honeybees on the ranch before we even arrived on the scene. Over the years he began adding to his bee colonies. The bee hives were up behind the house on the hill, perched on top of an old concrete cistern. Mom had seasonal allergies and had read a lot of articles about the miracle cures of honey. She decided that this was the remedy for all that ailed her and was raring to go. They bought all of the cool bee stuff, like the smokers that are supposed to make the bees drowsy so they don't notice when their honey is being stolen, the hats with the hoods to keep the bees from stinging faces or getting trapped in one's hair, the arm length leather gloves that were described in the catalog as sting proof, plus all the hive equipment. When they needed new bees for a hive, they were ordered straight from a bee catalog. The live bees were shipped to the very small local post office. They arrived in a full buzz in a narrow screened covered box. Inside of the crate, in the very center was a special little box that held the queen bee, as each hive requires a queen to be happy. The queen was sealed in her little throne room with royal jelly. The worker bees would eventually eat through the substance and free her from her cage. The master plan was to have the bees installed in their new home by the time this happened. It was a sure bet that as soon as that package arrived, our phone would start ringing. When we walked into the post office to pick them up, all we could hear was the sound of angry bees a-buzzing. It sounded just like something from an Alfred Hitchcock movie.

Harvesting the honey was quite an undertaking. First, the person or persons appointed to actually rob the hives had to gear up. The literature suggested wearing light colored clothing to keep the bees calm. Next, it was time to get the smokers going, which could be a bit of a challenge. We would load the contraptions up with old rags and get them burning. The trick was to have a significant smoky-fog emitted from the smoke stack on the smoker, without any actual flames shooting out to instantly fry the bees. The arm-length gloves were then tied to the upper arms to prevent adventurous bees from wiggling down into them. Finally, the hat and face net was donned. The hat resembled a safari hat and the net covered the face and neck. Since this was often done during the hotter months, the outfitted prospective bee robber would be in a real sweat even before approaching the bees. Now it was time to begin the serious job of stealing honey.

Walking up to an active bee hive was pretty scary even with all of the gear on. There was the constant angry buzzing of the bees and their attempts to attack through the protective gear. Carefully the smoke would be pumped into the hive in the hopes of making the bees calm and drowsy. Each section of the hive had to be slowly lifted off, being careful not to smash the bees whenever possible. The frames inside the hive were examined for honey comb. The ones with honey were removed and new frames were put back in to start the honey making process all over again. This seemed to be the time when that determined bee would find her way into the face net. The first warning was a loud buzzing in the ear. Nothing pisses a honeybee off more than being trapped. They go nuts and someone sure enough is going to get stung.

Once we had removed the frames with the honey, these were carried into the house. Inevitably, a few bees would come in with the honey, so we now had honeybees flying around kitchen. The honeycomb was cut into pieces with a heated knife and put down into clean jars. We would then smash the broken honeycomb to squeeze the honey out of it and pour it into the jars around the honeycomb. We always kept honey on the kitchen table year round. One time Mom tried to make candles from the leftover wax from the honeycomb, but she was not very successful. She really did hate to see anything go to waste.

If we didn't remove the honey often enough, the bees would feel they were finished at that home and head off for a new place. This is when they swarmed. One Sunday, I was in the hammock in the backyard. Sunday was the mandatory day of rest, unless Charles had something we needed to do. I became aware of a buzzing sound only to realize that one of the beehives was swarming, and they had chosen me as their new home. They were landing all over me. I carefully got out of the hammock trying not to make any sudden moves. The experts say that bees won't sting while swarming, but I did not think it was a good time to test that theory. It was summer and I was barefoot. Needless to say, I moved very slowly while brushing the bees off of me trying not to squash any of our flying friends.

Sometimes for sick entertainment, we would watch the honeybees aggravate the dogs. The buzzing would irritate the dogs to the point that they would suddenly snap at the bees, catching them in their mouths. Once the dogs started panting again, we could see the big welts on their tongues where the bees had stung them. Sometimes their long tongues would be decorated with 5 or 6 welts.

One right of passage for any country kid is that first time to try to smoke a cigarette. My first and last time was in a hayloft with a boy who was a couple of years older than me. He had matches and cigarettes stashed in the hayloft for his smoking experimentation. I am happy to say that I was a complete failure. I did almost set the hay on fire when I dropped the offending cigarette. To compound my stupidity, I confessed to my sisters, which led directly to a dreaded punishment by Mom and Charles. I swore off the smokes forever.

chapter 10

1969

It is hard to win the fight when the house in question is actually falling down around your ears. One morning at breakfast, we were sitting at the kitchen table when the ceiling in the front living room literally fell in. When the dust settled, there was no doubt as to what the next remodeling project would be. Our years in Tennessee were spent rebuilding one room after another. I don't think there was ever a time when we lived there, that the house was declared "finished." We quickly learned the art of demolition and remodeling as we advanced from one room to the next. Mom moved at what we referred to as "June Speed." She would hammer and saw things so quickly that if our fingers were not kept curled close to our hands, they would fall victim to her hammer or saw blade. We would methodically destroy one room and then rebuild it. When that room was completed, we would move onto the next. The old kitchen at the back was converted to a den. A porch on the back was made into a laundry room. A porch at the side was made into a mud room/pantry and we built a two car carport and full workshop on the back of the house. There were two airplane hangers and various other outbuildings. We literally built these with our own blood, sweat and tears. Even after we had moved on with our lives, whenever we would come home for a visit, there was always some addition / remodel project planned for this dilapidated plantation house.

There seemed to be an unending supply of people who would show up to work at the Flying M Ranch on any given day. Some of these were "regular" helpers who would work on the ranch several days a week. Others were kids from really sad home situations who needed money for their families, or needed a home-cooked meal. We were always cooking for an army, especially on Saturdays. Our kitchen would have been classified more as fast food instead of gourmet. In the tradition of the South, everything was deep fried if at all possible. We had this wicked deep fryer that would bubble out and over at the least provocation. The cook for the week would have spot burns on her arms where the grease would pop out and sear the skin. Of course, the cooking came after a hard morning of work, followed by cleaning up the kitchen while Charles took a nap on the couch. And then we went back to work to start all over again.

Ideally, on a ranch there are at least two roundups a year. We were lucky to get one in during a 12 month span. When it was time for the annual roundup, it took longer to catch the horses to ride in the cattle drive than it did to herd the cows. The rideable horses were kept in the front pasture. We would start early the day before the big event trying to catch them. We would spend hours chasing them back and forth in the front field. I swear they laughed when they galloped past us, just out of reach. We tried all of the usual baits like sweet feed or corn to lure them close to us. They would snatch a couple of bites and dash off before we could grab their halters. I think they finally let us catch them out of pity.

The big roundups were always an adventure. We would spend weeks working on the "corral" that consisted of several progressively smaller fenced areas, ending in a holding pen. In the last holding area, the cows were shooed one-by-one into a mobile cattle shoot. There were vaccinations and castrations for the calves, along with branding and tagging of the ears.

Roundups were nasty events. Excited cows tend to pee constantly and shoot out streams of diarrhea. This mixture was churned up by frantic hoofs into the mud in the corral. The result was a substance that would suck the boots right off of our feet. We spent half of the time trying not to get kicked or rammed by the excited cows, while other half was spent trying to pull our boots out of the manure / mud and slide them back on over our now-green socks.

Because the cows were unpredictable when infused with roundup adrenaline, there was always risk and danger involved. Charles instructed us to always look the cows in the eye and not show any fear. I always found that making the most noise was more effective in keeping them moving away from me than direct eye contact. One year, Nancy got mad at a calf that wasn't cooperating and kicked it as it ran by. The calf gave as good as it got by landing a direct hit under her chin that knocked her on her butt in the manure. I think I saw him smiling as he ran back to his momma.

Charles got the notion that the real money was to be made in hogs. Naturally, this required a huge initial investment in all kinds of special pig equipment and the construction of special pens. For some reason, he had decided to have us build the pigpen up at Cave Springs, about a mile from the house. Pigs are pretty dumb animals and require a lot of supervision and care. Because the pen was so far from the house, there was no way to properly watch the pigs. And the piglets were easy prey. Their mothers would eat them or crush them; buzzards would fly down and scoop the piglets up for dinner to go, and anyone who wanted a free pig or two could take their sweet time in selecting. After the pig population had decreased by two thirds, the pig pen was moved to a more remote location in the woods. This was still too far away from the house to monitor the pigs. At the new location, the wandering wildlife and dogs had ready access to a warm pork dinner.

We did have pig killings every once in awhile. These were started early in the morning. Charles had a boom truck that had an elevated hook on the back. He would drive this to the pig pen with a loaded gun. The unsuspecting target would come up to the fence expecting to be fed, not to become part of the food chain. With a quick blast to the head, the deed was done. Quickly, the hog had to be attached by a chain around his back feet to the boom hook and suspended into the air. With a quick slice, Charles would slit its throat, so that all of the blood would gush out on the way home. At the house, a fifty gallon drum would be ready and waiting, filled with water and heated to boiling with a fire underneath. The carcass would be dunked repeatedly into the smoldering makeshift pot. As soon as it was pulled out, we would get to work quickly, shaving off the hair with knives. The stench from the boiling water, blood and pig filth was enough to make me rethink my breakfast choices. When Charles decided that we had gotten the skin scraped clean enough, then the heavy corpse would be laid out on a nearby table and the serious work of gutting and dividing would commence. The head would be severed and set off to the side where it would watch in wide-eyed wonder. Local people would start showing up to get any parts that we might not want. In the country, every part of the swine would be used. Pig brains, chitins, fried pork skins, pig's feet, and not to forget the mountain oysters. (These were considered such a delicacy that if we were castrating the pigs in the pasture, eager farmers would help hold the pig for the promise of the gonads.) We would be up to our elbows in blood as we separated the different cuts of pork and packaged them up for the freezer and a future dinner.

One summer, Nancy rescued the runt of a litter from certain death. She raised the little guy on a bottle and named him Aaron. When she first brought him home, he would easily fit in the palm of her hand. As he grew, he took up residence in an old dog house behind the house. Aaron prospered with her love and care and soon grew into a 200 + pound boar that still wanted to climb in her lap for some loving. He was a big ol' hawg. One day, that little pig was sent off to market. We learned early on to be careful with our love, as our pets could be the next entrée on the dinner table.

One of Charles' favorite things to yell at us on the farm was "Think! Think! Think!" He said that thinking was the hardest job of all, but it sure looked pretty easy from our side of the workbench. I think that was his excuse for being slack-ass lazy. We were also never allowed to put our hands on our hips. If we dared to take this appalling stance, we would be rewarded with a blow to the head. Apparently it reminded him of a pose that his ex-wife often took with him and he would not tolerate it. He also believed that kids who were working would not get into trouble, so he made sure to have plenty of work for us. He liked to say that if he ran out of things for us to do, he would just have us dig a hole in the ground and then fill it back in. And I think he meant it.

One of those jobs he loved to have us do was to go into the fields to pick up rocks. We spent lifetimes wandering around the fields in the hot summer sun, throwing rocks into the back of an old beat-up Scout pickup. After we had picked up a load of rocks, we then got to unload the rocks into whatever designated area Charles might have that day. We built bridges across ditches, filled in gullies, and shoved rocks into ground-hog holes in the pasture. All of this was done in the relentless heat while combating the red ants, stinging insects, biting horse flies, snakes, and the renegade rocks. It seemed inevitable that during this task, someone would either get hit with a stray rock (usually in the head) or another window in the pickup would get broken. It was a good time to let out some pent-up hostilities and pretend it was an accident.

Another task that had to be done every few years was the digging of the septic tank. The location for this smelly receptacle was directly in front of the house. We had to dig a huge hole in the middle of the front lawn large enough to hold three metal fifty gallon drums. These were riddled with holes and connected to the drainage system from the house. We then filled the hole back in with dirt. The waste from the house would work its way to the drums where it would ferment, while the liquid refuse would leak out into the yard. Without a doubt, the grass was always greener over the septic tank, but the air sure wasn't sweeter. The smell of raw sewage was always waiting to settle around us like a wet blanket when we stepped outside. If our path took us through the greener grass, we would sink down into the seepage that would ooze into our shoes. Heaven forbid that we be barefoot; it would be like walking foot-naked through a pigpen.

Junior was a special billy goat that became part of our menagerie around about this time. He was an orphan and Nancy became his surrogate mother. Junior was adorable as a kid, but he quickly grew into a wild and crazy guy. He had a set of horns that were probably three to four feet across by the time he was full grown buck. He was also very fragrant in a way that only billy goats can be. Just the memory of that aroma makes my eyes water. On rainy days, we could literally smell the goat herd hours before they actually arrived in the back pasture at the house. It didn't take Junior long to figure out that he had a pretty good life living with his people family. His attempts to mingle with the herd were unsuccessful. They openly rejected him and Junior did not handle rejection very well. He had a tendency to be psychotic and aggressive. When he was in one of his fits, as we liked to call them, he would stick his tongue out of the side of his mouth and bite it while letting out horrific noises. Because of his erratic behavior, his extensive horns and his love to butt things, he had to be chain to a tree to protect people and property. Junior's days were spent butting a wooden swing suspended from his staked-out tree until there was barely a sliver of wood left.

During that memorable summer, Charles hired a young guy to help with the airplane repair and renovations. This was the year that the High Karate cologne debuted. This young man would liberally apply this cologne each morning before coming to work. And dear ol' Junior was driven absolutely mad by this scent. He would go into a frenzy whenever he got a whiff of it. One day this chap was working under a plane that we had just refinished and were in the process of reassembling. Junior broke lose from his chain and made a bee-line for this unsuspecting male. He literally attacked this guy under the plane, which resulted in several rips and tears in the fabric from his horns. We couldn't laugh at the time, but I still smile when I either see a picture of Junior in all of his horniness or get a whiff of High Karate cologne.

Not long after, on one fateful day, Junior lunged one too many times at the end of his chain and snapped his neck. Charles dictated that we had to get him buried before Nancy could leave to perform in an evening band concert at the school. At this point in time, we were still sentimental enough to take the time and effort to lovingly bury our pets on the side of the hill. (Time in Tennessee would quickly cure us from this sweet, idealistic and back-breaking ritual.) As a result, there were a lot of sink-holes in the side of the hill where the dirt would settle in, after you-know. We quickly guesstimated the width and depth of the plot for Junior's body, but failed to dig deep enough to accommodate his horns. For many years to come, Junior would literally trip me up when I would go running down that hill and catch my foot on his horn that was sticking out of the ground by about 5 inches.

While summer evaporated around us, we had many things to keep us busy and out of trouble. There was bush-hogging to do, cows to round up, buildings and barns to repair, fencing to be done, trees to be cleared, pigs to be castrated, airplanes to be refinished, animals to take care of, vehicles and tractors to repair, rocks to pick up, lumber to be cut and the garden. The garden for some reason became my responsibility. My mother believed that if we were going to plant a garden, then we just might as well plant a huge one.

Mom had always wanted a genuine in-ground swimming pool and Charles decided that he would fulfill that dream for her. One year, the railroad was building a dirt ramp "downtown" so that dump trucks could drive up the incline and dump dirt into the railroad cars. The dirt they were transporting held some type of mineral that there was a market for. Charles worked out an arrangement with the railroad to have them dig the dirt out of our backyard for their ramp for free; under the condition they would also dig a hole for Mom's dream swimming pool. In the process, they dug a big chunk out of the hill that was once the backyard behind the house. It was on top of this dug-out hill that Mom decided to plant her dream garden.

It was my responsibility to keep this enormous patch of earth watered, picked and free from weeds and pests. Mom bought one of those Troy Built rototillers that felt like it weighed a million tons. I tipped the scales at about 69 pounds at the time. If the tiller hit a rock, or just decided that it was going to head to higher ground, there was not much that I could do to change its mind. It was like wrestling with an angry bull. Sometimes it would plow under half a row of corn before I could get the crazy thing stopped.

Then there was the nightmare of harvesting. Once the vegetables started to ripen, we would have bushels of tomatoes, beans, okra, taters, peas, corn, lettuce, carrots, and everything else all at the same time. If they made a seed for it, then my mom had us planting it. Half the time, I didn't even know what the plants were supposed to look like when they were first sprouting. To my eyes, they all looked like weeds. It was a sun-up to sun-down job in the fierce summer heat.

The absolute worse thing to harvest was okra, which must be experienced to be appreciated. The actual vegetable has some kind of spines on it so that if picked without gloves on, the spines get imbedded under in the skin and causes the commencement of relentless itching. Nothing but time can ease this endless torture. I scoured up some long lavender evening gloves from the old dress-up clothes in the attic. I don't know which ancestor they belonged to, but I doubt that they ever imagined their finery would end up as okra-pickin' garden gloves.

In order to reach the garden perched on the top of this hill, I had to trudge up a narrow, twisting path that wound its way along the side of the hill. It was a real juggling act to keep the full cart from plummeting over the edge on the downhill trip. Though there were numerous vegetable casualties over the years, miraculously I always managed to keep a firm footing on the path.

To add to the challenge, the path to the garden went right past the bee hives. Each trip to or from the garden was risky, depending what kind of mood the bees might be in. If they were cranky, I was sure to get attacked while maneuvering the narrow garden path. The bees would often get trapped in my hair during their attack and would work themselves into a frenzy when they couldn't escape from the hairy net. My only alternative was to smash them against my skull to kill them before they could sting me. It took much coordination to try to maneuver a cart full of round vegetables down a twisting and winding path while smacking myself upside the head to kill the bees trapped in my hair.

When I finally got the vegetables down to the house, the next phase of gardening started. The vegetables all had to be cleaned and prepared for canning or freezing. This would take hours of redundant work. Mom did not feel that we were prepared for winter unless the pantry was full of jars and the freezer was full to bursting. I would be up into the wee hours of the morning waiting for the canners to finish and the lids to pop on top of the jars.

Then it was time to repeat the process the next day. I am disturbed to find that even at my advanced age, I am still inflicted with a compulsion to pull stray weeds and pick anything ripe in my vicinity.

We always seemed to have a multitude of mangy dogs on the farm. They were kept tied up in various places around the property. As the dog population grew, the novelty of having our own special dog faded. Charles did not believe in having pets spayed or neutered, so there always seem to be some kind of puppies around under foot. (Interestingly, he did not have a problem with drowning unwanted puppies. It was the surgical sterilization that he found to be incompatible with his religious beliefs.) It became my job to feed all of these dogs. At one point I was feeding at least nine grown dogs with who-knows how many puppies. We kept the dry dog food in the back of the now abandoned horse trailer. The food was stored in metal trashcans to keep it dry. The problem with this system was that the lids were easily bent or warped, which meant they no longer had a tight seal on the receptacles. As a result, every time I opened up the trashcan to scoop out the dog food, I never knew what kind of surprises I would find trapped inside. Often it would be a mouse or two, hopping around in a panic, desperately trying to climb up the slippery sides to freedom. This problem required hunting down a cat; putting it into the trashcan; closing the lid and waiting about five minutes. That is one way of recycling on a farm. Sometimes the surprise could be more gruesome, like a snake, which probably crawled into the trashcan to eat the mice. When that happened, I just got the heck out of Dodge.

One of Mom's money saving ideas was to pick up any road kill that we would pass on the road to bring home for the dogs to eat. She got extra excited over rabbits. This was an especially gruesome task in the summer when the carcass would have cooked a bit on the hot asphalt before we would happen upon it. Some of the body parts were usually smashed from tire contact, but Mom didn't care. I especially minded picking it up if it was infested with flies and / or maggots. We would toss the road-kill morsel in the floorboard of the car. It was imperative to remember to get it out when we got home or it could get smelly really fast. The dogs would snatch them right out of our fingers and chew on them for hours. By the time they were finished, there wouldn't even be a whisper of a bunny tail left.

For some unknown reason, Charles was obsessed with International Harvester vehicles. He would tolerate no other brand of cars or trucks on the ranch for years. Therefore, the three of us all drove International Scouts, which were like an un-cool jeep-type vehicle. Basically, they were metal boxes with engines, which were always reluctant to crank. Of course, they had the standard two seats up front. However, some of them had only metal ledges along the sides in the back for any extra passengers, with absolutely no padding, whatsoever. These vehicles had no AC for the summer and the heaters didn't do much in the winter. I have distinct memories of a fried backside sitting on that metal seat in the summer and frostbite in the winter. They were hard and uncomfortable year round. We were required to check the engine oil and the air in our tires each time before we were allowed to drive off, and we had to grease all the universal joints on a regular basis.

The day Beth reached the magic age of 16, Mom took her to the DMV and she got her driver's license. She now became the official driver for Mom and Charles. She was our chauffeur back and forth to school in Alabama, which meant that we were flying low to the ground instead of up in the air. She also had to be the substitute mom in town, picking me up from dance and doing all of the grocery shopping and errands for Mom. Acquiring a driver's license meant more chores, responsibilities, and headaches.

One of my favorite memories of teenager Beth was one of the times she was doing the grocery shopping for the ranch. Mom would make up these ridiculously long grocery lists. The groceries would completely fill at least one cart and might actually require a second to hold all the items. I was shopping with Beth and we were in a race to finish and make the 30 minute drive home. We were about halfway through the list when Beth realized that she didn't have the checkbook. Other than cash, this was the primary means of payment in those days. She was already mortified by the prospect of having to purchase this ridiculous amount of groceries each week in a store where her peers worked and watched. To not have the check book was an extra humiliation. We were in the middle of the canned vegetables when she made the discovery. She promptly left the cart in the middle of the store and made a beeline for the door. I was flabbergasted with her abrupt abandonment of our groceries. When I began to ask out loud what she was doing, she grabbed my arm and jerked me along behind her.

Another grocery memoir involved Nancy. She had developed a fascination for animal skeletons and bones. These, of course, were always in ready supply on the farm. For some unknown reason, Nancy had stashed a bunch of huge horse bones under the passenger seat of the Scout. Imagine the bag-boy's surprise when he was helping to put the groceries in the car and flipped the seat up only to uncover the skeletal remains of a large mammal. He had a startled look on his face, but he never asked who, what or why.

chapter 11

1970

About three years after the large hole for the swimming pool was dug, Charles was finally ready to get on with the building of the actual structure. The pool-hole had ample time to fill with rainwater over the years, while the ducks had laid claim to it as the perfect pond. They had done what all ducks do while swimming around; lots of pooping and dropping eggs to rot.

School work and homework were to be completed at school, so that we could work from the time we got home until after sundown. All of the work on the ranch, including the construction of the pool was done after school and on weekends. When we got started on the pool, the first step was to pump all of the water out of the dirt hole. This took several days. Next, we had to shape the mud on the bottom by hand into the desired shape for the pool bottom. We were covered from head to foot with mud (and duck poop) while attempting to gain some footing in the sticky muck to form the sides. While slipping and sliding around, we inadvertently uncovered countless rotten eggs either by scooping them up with the mud in our hands, or by stepping on them. To this day, the stench of rotten eggs triggers a severe emotional response from this childhood nightmare. While we were literally digging this pool by hand, Charles would either lie on the grass on his side or sit in a chair under an umbrella while he "supervised". He said that he was "thinking" which required much more energy than what we were doing. Yeah, right.

The next stage was construction of a grid on the bottom with metal rods to hold the concrete. This took days to complete as each junction had to be welded. Then came the "Big Day". I can't remember how many truck loads of cement were poured that day, but the flow of concrete seemed endless. It was a cloudy day and was drizzling, but that didn't matter. Once the order had been placed, there was no backing out. We worked in wet concrete nonstop for the entire day. It got splashed down inside our shoes, boots and gloves. By the end of the day, we had chemical burns on various body parts from the contact with our skin.

After the cement dried, it was now time to build the sides of the pool. This wasn't just any old concrete pond, but would be an Olympic-sized pool by dimensions and nightmares. We worked for hours each day hauling cinder blocks and concrete. The concrete was stirred in a mixer on the back of the tractor and the demand for this wet nasty substance seemed endless. We had to work well after dark, often until 11 pm or later, which made it hard to get up for school the next day at 5:30 am. The construction of this pool seemed to take forever. After the concrete construction was finished, the entire structure was then plastered by hand. It was a bit tricky trying to get the plaster to stick to the perpendicular block walls. Next came the painting with the white epoxy paint. Painting with epoxy paint in the bottom of a 14 foot pool in the hot Tennessee sun left us all feeling a little buzzed and carefree. The fume cloud hovered in our workspace, literally enveloping us. The walkway around the edge of the pool also had to be painted. To keep it from being slippery as ice when wet, we mixed sand into the epoxy paint before applying. The end result was a concrete path that would tear the skin right off of bare feet because the sand particles were so rough. We apparently were a little heavy handed with adding the sand to the mixture.

Charles designed some funky type of filter system for the pool that used Diatomaceous earth and long poles with round filter disks attached. Cleaning the pump system meant that we had to climb down inside these three pits and lift the filters out to be hosed off on a regular basis. This was a nasty chore because the green slime and trash caked on the disks would drip all over us during the lifting out phase.

The next project was construction of a diving platform. This was shaped out of metal plumbing pipe fitted together with connecting joints. The diving board was a recycled job, so it also got painted with the epoxy and sand mixture like the walkway. Its abrading surface would buff the calluses right off of our feet.

The pool was a nightmare to keep clean, and always had frogs, tadpoles, snakes and other critters in it. There was no way to cover it during the winter, so it would get filled with leaves and debris that would take weeks to fish out. Until the day that I drove away from the house for the last time, I could never look at that pool with any kind of enjoyment or appreciation. It represented a nightmare that we had somehow survived.

Haying time in the hot summer sun was a misery that can only be appreciated by those who have experienced it. I am not talking about the big round hay bales that farmers use today. These were the little rectangular ones that city people use to decorate their yards in the fall. If the rains were good and we were unlucky, hay time came twice in a summer. Average temperatures during the summer days of my childhood were in the triple digits. Add in the southern humidity, and hay days were hot and wretched. Rarely was there any kind of wind or breeze. Before we even got started good, we were slick with sweat.

As haying time approached, the weather was monitored closely. When the weather man predicted a dry spell for several days, the plan of attack was carefully laid out. It was imperative for the hay to be dry when it was baled because wet hay could lead to two major problems: baled wet hay could begin to smolder and self-combust, burning down the barn with all of the hay, or the wet hay could mold, causing the farm animals to get deathly sick when they ate it.

One person had to drive the tractor with the cutting blade. This seemed like a cake job until the hidden obstacles in the field were factored in. The cutting blade stuck straight out from the tractor, skimming along the ground. This meant that the hay was cut as close to the ground as possible to avoid any waste. Because the hay was tall, there was limited visibility. This job required alertness at all times for obstacles in the path of the tractor and any stumps, rocks or animals (living or dead) that might damage the cutting blade. The driver also had to contend with all kinds of flying insects who were ticked off with the disturbance of their homes. Many times this insect force consisted of yellow jackets that made their nests in the ground. Talk about distractions... It was a dreaded deed to have to drive back to the house and report that the blade had gotten damaged. Time was lost in the repair and no matter what, the blame for any delays or lost hay would come back to haunt us.

With perfect conditions, the hay would dry quickly and the next step would begin. The second tractor driver (it worked best with at least two tractors) would run the hay rake. I was always fascinated by this piece of farm equipment. It would scoop up the loose hay and toss it around. This would help to dry the hay and then it would spit it out the end in a windrow. This nice long fluffy line of hay made it easier to be picked up by the baler.

Step three was the baling machine. This operator also had to be ever vigilant for the dreaded obstacles that could be picked up by the baler and get into the inner workings of the machine, causing major damage. There were lots of moving parts in the baler that would take large of amounts of time and money to repair. This contraption picked up the loose hay and by some miracle, not only was the hay compacted when it came out the other end, if we were really lucky, it would actually have two strings tied around it for easy pickup. We often found surprises in the hay bales, like small rodents or snakes. One year we even had a cat that survived a baling. He was known as Baler from that time on and lived to a ripe old age.

Now was the worst part of the entire process. We would drive trucks around behind the hay baler and pick up the individual hay bales. It was a real struggle when we were working with a tall truck, because the bales had to be thrown up to the person on the back of the truck to catch. I learned at an early age that no matter how hot the weather was during hay season, long pants and a long sleeved shirt were a must. We sweated like a sinner at a revival, but the long clothing protected our arms and legs from the scratchy hay. Any exposed skin would be quickly abraded by the straw. Once scratched, the gnats, flies and other insects would swoop in to feast on our blood, while the sweat oozed into the wounds. It still brings a tear to my eye to remember the sting of it.

By the time we got the truck full, we were pretty much exhausted. There was a short ride on the top of the hay, back to the barn where the work started all over again, in reverse. While unloading the bales into the hayloft, we were working in the shade of the barn, but there was little, if any, air movement. Taking a deep breath only resulted in filling up our lungs with all the hay particles and dust floating around in the air. The bales had to be thrown up into the loft from the back of the truck. Anther person was responsible for stacking the bales in the hayloft. This was a very important job. It was imperative to get some type of grid / stacking technique going, or the hay bales would tumble over when they got to a certain height. A good stacker could get the hay all the way to the roof with no leaning of the bales.

One of the trademarks of barns on the Flying M Ranch was that they all had hazardous haylofts. The floors resembled Swiss cheese. There was no maintenance or repairs done to the barns, so when the wood rotted, we either left a hole that a body could fall through or we threw something over it. There seemed to be an endless supply of loose wooden doors around the ranch. Maybe they came from the deserted houses around there, or maybe people just didn't use doors. For whatever reason, in any given hayloft, there might be 3 or 4 wooden doors carefully positioned over hazardous booby traps. If we had to shift them for some reason (perhaps to cover another hole) hundreds of mice would swarm out from underneath them. It was important to resist the urge to jump around or the mice would be squashed under our feet.

Rats were also a contention in the haylofts. Once, we were loading hay in one of the barns and a huge rat came running out. It was bigger than a cat and was running straight towards me. At the last minute it veered away from me, but not before I had needed a change of underwear.

During the winter, the hay process was reversed to feed the cows and horses. Because the cows liked to stand around the barns where the hay was kept, the entire area around the barn would be one big wet manure pit. It would be so deep, that unless the truck had four-wheel drive, we couldn't get close enough to the barn to load the hay out of the hayloft without getting stuck. We spent precious time in the bitter cold walking the bales out to dry ground where the truck was, while trying to keep the bales away from the hungry cows and attempting to keep our boots on our feet. The cold wet manure would act like a vacuum, sucking the boots right off our feet. One fateful step and we now had cold, wet, smelly socks **and** a missing boot. It took great coordination to balance on one foot while trying to locate the missing boot, get it back on, and keep the ravenous cows from ripping the hay bales out of our hands.

chapter 12

1971

Beth graduated from Athens High School in 1971. That summer, we had a burden to hold a revival in Prospect. Our pastor at our church in Athens agreed to preach at our event, and we began to plan in earnest. The entire thing was planned by teenagers with a heart for Christ. We put up the fliers and got the word out. It was held up at the Prospect School with an improvised stage set up on the flat bed of one of the farm trucks for two nights only. We even put a piano on the back of the truck for music. The chairs were borrowed from the Prospect funeral home. Most people came out of curiosity. It was almost like a drive-in movie because a lot of people just sat in their vehicles or on the hoods of their cars and listened. On the last night of the revival, our next-door neighbor came forward during the invitation and gave his heart to Christ. It was one of those amazing things that happen rarely in life. I swear, we could almost see Christ in his face. He did a complete 180 in his life. He stopped drinking, swearing and abusing his family. Less than 2 weeks later, he was killed in a car accident while still a young man. I get chills when I think about how that revival event was for him. I know that other people made decisions, but it was his last chance at salvation and he embraced it with his whole heart.

Meanwhile, Charles came up with another new plan to make the big money. He decided that we were going to raise bottle-fed calves that he would buy at the cattle auction. Dairy farmers often sold their calves to avoid the expense of feeding and raising them. Charles spent hundreds of dollars on special pens and feeders. In the very first year of this endeavor, all of the bottle calves got the pinkeye. Some of the cases were so severe that it actually caused their eyeballs to change shape and the corneas became pointed. One calf's eyes were so diseased that she ended up being totally blind. Beth formed a special bond with this calf and named her Baby. Baby would run towards the sound of Beth's voice, knowing that she would have a treat for her. Of course, when Baby reached the goal weight, that little calf went off to market. A few years later, the pens and feeders joined the graveyard of rusting equipment left sitting in the fields.

Beth began getting ready for college. She enrolled at Tennessee Tech, which was about 3 hour drive from Prospect. Charles liked to say that Beth was the apple of his eye. This sounds like a compliment, but considering the source, it was really kind of sick. Beth was the most normal and social of the three of us; probably because she had benefited from those early years in a functional family. After she left for college, Charles became aware of the fact that his power and control was limited to direct contact. He realized that if we left the ranch, we would be out of his scope of control. The rules and regulations began multiplying and changing daily for Nancy and me. We never knew what new law Charles would dream up and what impact it would have on our so called lives. He became consumed with the idea that Beth was going "wild" at college. He hired a private investigator to spy on her and when the report showed nothing of concern, Charles only became more convinced that she was up to no good. Mom and Charles would call her up at college and demand that she come home right away, even if it meant she would be missing her classes. When she got home, Charles would remove the distributor cap from her car so that she couldn't leave until he was good and ready. Poor Beth was being jerked back and forth constantly by Charles throughout her freshman year.

Nancy was now the designated transporter to and from school. She assumed all of the other duties, plus the errands to town for parts and to pick up feed and items for the animals. Yep, being licensed meant that we had added responsibilities and duties along with all of the regular chores. Nancy got promoted to the chair next to Charles at the dinner table when Beth left for college. This would prove to be the most hazardous place to sit. About twice a week, Charles would rise up like a tidal wave and knock her to the floor or bounce her off of the wall for no reason other than the fact that she lived and breathed. (I carefully watched all of this in my years next to the toaster and chose not to "move-up" to that seat when Nancy left for college. I decided that it was best to stay out of his arm's reach. That way I had a little warning if he was coming after me and could at least make an attempt to run.)

Charles was a firm believer that if he spared the rod, he would spoil the child. For sure, there were no spoiled children in his household. Charles really hated Nancy and she was often the recipient of his anger. There was just no way to predict what would set him off. Sometimes it would be just the way we held our heads that would trigger him. We were living in a constant state of fear. It was like being locked in a dark room with a rattlesnake. We never knew when or where he would strike next. There were the blows to the head, slaps across the face and then the beatings with belts or sticks until we literally could not sit down.

Breakfast was always the time when Charles took the shine off of the day. He never failed to administer his daily dose of verbal abuse. He repeatedly told us what failures and sinners we were, and how we would never amount to anything. One of his favorite barbs was "I'm going to laugh my head off when you get out in the world and fall flat on your face." Like Lucifer's own, he never missed an opportunity to tell us how ugly and unlovable we were. We heard these words so often that he became a continuous chanting in our heads about our failures and flaws. He intimidated, terrorized, punished and abused us, using religion as his weapon. Charles was fanatical in his daily devotions and prayers that we had to suffer through each and every morning. He had complete and utter control over how long this ritual would last and the more we were rushed to get somewhere (like school), the slower he would pray. He dominated every aspect of our lives. It was psychological warfare with few survivors. And Mom stood by and let him do it.

After the car wreck, Nancy absolutely hated to have her picture taken. She had suffered a lot of facial trauma and had several scars as a result. When faced with having her picture taken, she would get into a real funk. She would put on her grumpy face and there was no snapping her out of it until she was ready. These moods usually coincided with the day that we were to take pictures for the annual Christmas letter. The holiday newsletter was Mom's yearly contact with the people from her past. She wanted the pictures to look like we were living the high life in Tennessee and were one big happy family. One of the more memorable picture days involved Nancy posing on the tractor. (Mom's idea). Nancy did not want to smile and refused to put on a happy face for the camera. The blows that Charles delivered to her head and face incredibly did not improve her mood or make her more inclined to grin. That year the Christmas letter had a picture of Beth looking sophisticated and happy; me, posed with my hands over the keys on the piano and a smile on my face; and Nancy, sitting on the tractor with tear streaks on her cheeks and bruises on her face. Merry Christmas!

After Beth left for college, Charles became more antisocial and was unable to get along with others. He began to realize that it was only a matter of time before his labor force would leave. One day, Charles decreed that it was no longer acceptable for us to wear pants. He chanted the required out-of-context scripture verse to support his claim. Since we had to work like men on his ranch, wearing a dress would have been impractical and immodest. He decided that we would wear pants but with a skirt over top of them. Nancy took her overalls and sewed a "skirt" to them at the waist. I found an old pleated plaid skirt that I slit up the seam and pinned around my waist over top of my raggedy pants. This unfashionable look really set us apart from everyone else. It was another way to humiliate and isolate us. I am not gonna' lie; it was a hard life for a teenager.

Charles was also becoming increasingly paranoid and squirrelly. He was convinced that the entire community was waiting for the perfect moment to siphon gas from the planes, rustle cows, take our precious hay, or steal his tools. When we all left the house together, like to go to church, Nancy or I had to hide in the floorboard of the car. (Remember that this is where our shoes and boots covered with manure rested and where Mom liked to stash her road kill.) We would be all cleaned up, in our Sunday best when he would decide which one of us would be the lucky one. And it wasn't like we were only down there for a few minutes. We had to crouch down there for at least 15 minutes, until we were halfway to church and he decided that the coast was clear. If we were not crouched down low enough, he would reach over the seat and give us a smack on the back of our heads. His rational for this was that if "someone" was waiting for us to leave for church, they would count heads in the car and realize that someone was missing and could possibly still be at the ranch. We also had to take the phone off of the hook at the house when we left. Back in those days, when the phone was left off of the hook for an extended length of time, anyone trying to call would get a busy signal. The problem was remembering to hang the phone back up when we got home.

This was also the German Shepherd phase. What could make a better guard dog than a German shepherd? Charles bought a registered matched breeding pair named Brock and Mandy. Poor Mandy would crank out a litter of puppies every few months. Charles didn't believe in selling the puppies based on some scripture verse. As a result, the entire community had lots of "registered" German Shepherds. Brock outlived Mandy by several years and became the appointed watchdog on the ranch, probably due to his unpredictable "sic 'em" personality. He was staked out on a chain next to an old International station wagon that was up on cinder blocks. This was his dog house, year round. We had tried to give it a homier feel by putting up boards around the perimeter of the abandoned car. This didn't give Brock much protection from the elements, but the boards did provide endless entertainment for him   His days were spent carrying these boards around in his mouth as far as his chain would reach. He devoted hours to moving them back and forth. When he tired of this activity, he would chew them up.

Understandably, Brock had a lot of pent up hostilities because he was chained up almost 24/7. Sundays were the exception. When we left for church, he was untied and left to roam the ranch. He would plot all week for these few hours of freedom. When we would come home from church, we would find any number of dead pets and animals. He was like the doggy mafia. He had quite an impressive hit list over the years: numerous goats, geese, ducks, calves…. and most of them were my precious pets.

Since the ducks had been displaced with the installation of the in-ground swimming pool, Mom had us dig a smaller pond for them behind the house. She was fascinated with using duck eggs to cook with. After all, one duck egg was equal to two chicken eggs. (If you could find the eggs before they rotted.) She decided that if duck eggs were good, then goose eggs would be even better. Unfortunately, she did not factor in the unfriendly and aggressive personality of the general goose population. The meanest of our flock was a gray gander who believed he was the king of the pond and no one was to trespass into his territory. He did not even make exceptions for those of us (me) who had the unfortunate responsibility of feeding these ungrateful feathered birdbrains. He would carefully wait until I had one arm busy balancing the duck food and the other one wrapped around the post trying to unhook the chain to the gate before he would pounce. He would clamp down onto my arm and twist with all of his might, leaving both his mark and a lasting impression. After a few attacks like this, I carefully planned my retaliation. I left the food in the trashcan to free up that arm to use as a shield. When I reached inside to unlatch the gate, he was waiting for me. He launched towards my tender chicken wing, only to be snatched up in mid-snap by his long neck. I swung him around the top of my head about three times before catapulting him across the duck pond where he landed in the mud. He sat there a minute while he untwisted his neck and gave me a long hard look. He slowly waddled away and never ever tried to pull a plug out of my arm again.

Some months later, we came home from church one Sunday afternoon to find the old gray gander dead in the yard where killer Brock had eliminated him. Frugal Mom decided that it wasn't too late to try to cook him for lunch. The meat was a direct reflection of the old gray gander – tough, stringy and resistant. I found that I wasn't very hungry that day.

chapter 13

1972

In all our growing up years, Charles didn't spend one penny on us. The Social Security checks went to buy groceries and clothes. The trust funds took care of any medical expenses, braces, dance lessons, piano lessons, cars and more. Over time, Charles quickly and methodically siphoned off Mom's part of the Dad's life insurance. In the first year of their marriage, Charles constantly "borrowed" money from Mom. She wrote check after check to him. She would staple his worthless IOU's to these "loans". He never paid a penny of this money back, but systematically bled her dry financially.

Once Charles had Mom's money in his clutches, it just wasn't enough. He then began to plan ways to get his hands on our trust funds. His first victim was Beth. He convinced her that the best investment she could make was property. He persuaded her to buy a tract of land that conveniently bordered his ranch. She was only 19 at the time and a full-time college student.

Her trust fund money was used to make the down payment on the farm that she named "The Lazy B". Charles co-signed the note, which meant that if she wasn't able to make the monthly payments, then the loan would go under his name, and she would lose her investment. Of course, since she was hundreds of miles away at college, there was no way that she could keep up with a herd of cattle and make the payments. That meant the easy addition of 100 acres to the Flying M Ranch.

Charles was now into the bus ministry. This required purchasing an old school bus to drive along the back roads between Tennessee and Alabama, picking people up for church along the way. Sunday was the longest day of the week for us, as the bus route took about an hour and a half each way and we made this trip twice each Sunday. After church on Sunday nights we would stop at the Dixie Drive-in at the edge of town in Athens. Everyone was treated to one item off the menu. (Kind of like a bribe for coming to church.) It was my job to take the orders, purchase the items and then deliver them to the respective bus riders. I developed an intense dislike for soft-serve ice cream cones because they would always be melted by the time I got them back on the bus.

Goats on the Flying M Ranch had the lifespan of a soap bubble, thanks to Brock-the-dog and his love for killing things that were near and dear to our hearts. He watched us throughout the week and any animals that got our special attention were moved to the top of his hit list. As the number of dead pets increased, it became unrealistic to continue to bury them. We started dumping their remains in a ditch out in one of the pastures that we aptly named "the Ditch of Broken Dreams." This became a landmine of skeletal remnants of all shapes and sizes and a feeding ground for the buzzards. But some of the special pets were disposed of in more creative ways.

As my love for goats grew, I decided that I wanted to buy my very own pair. I purchased a nanny and a billy of the milk goat variety. I constructed a shed behind the house where I would lock them up whenever we left the farm to keep them safe. One fateful Sunday, Brock literally ripped the boards and wire off of the door to the shed to gain access to my pets. My precious nanny, Sassafras, was his victim that day. Nancy and I were told to get rid of her carcass and we were trying to do it as quickly as possible. We came up with a great plan to throw her off of the single lane bridge. (I have not doubts in my now older and wiser age, that this probably violated several laws. Ignorance is bliss; the saying goes, especially for teenagers.) Making sure the coast was clear, we parked the Scout in the middle of the bridge. There was much concern on our part about getting caught doing this and also getting stuck on the bridge with a car coming in the opposite direction. Sassafras was not only a large goat; she was also a well fed goat. Add rigor mortis, bloating, and dead weight (pun intended) to the equation and we had a pretty heavy problem on our hands. We drug her carcass out of the back of the Scout to the edge of the bridge. The swirling brown water of the river was several feet below. When we went to shove her off of the bridge, just as she was sliding so nicely into space, her rear hoof got caught in the metal edge. She began to swing by her trapped foot like a pendulum back and forth, dangling several feet above the water. At that precise moment, we heard a vehicle approaching. We quickly donned innocent expressions, jumped in the truck and drove off of the bridge. The driver must not have seen anything suspicious, because he continued on his way. By this time, we were in a near panic. We turned around and headed back onto the bridge. All we had in the back of the Scout was a dull ax. We began hacking away at her foot, so that she could have the burial at sea that I had envisioned. When she finally plunged into the river, we decided this would be our last watery burial. We took the easy way after that and dumped the rest of the pets in the Ditch of Broken Dreams.

One memorable day, Nancy, Mom and I were all crowded into the front of the hay truck. I, being the smallest, was squashed in between them on the seat. Mom told Nancy to roll down her window and call the cows. We had a very catchy phrase to summon the cows to dinner that went something like "Wooo Cowwww…. Suck…Suck… Suck…" I have no idea who created this chant, but the sound of those words sung out into the country air made the cows salivate and hoof it to the barn. (Kinda like Pavlov's dog trick but with larger mammals.) On this particular day, Nancy did not feel like calling the cows and told Mom that it was dumb and she wasn't going to do it. Mom yelled at Nancy and told her to roll down her window and call the cows. Nancy (being Nancy) again refused. By this time, I was starting to sweat because I was trapped in between them. Mom parked the truck and lost it. She started smacking Nancy. However, I was the one getting the brunt of the beating because the elbow of Mom's swinging arm was making contact with me before her hand was making contact with Nancy's hard head. Mom then jumped out of the truck and went around to Nancy's door, at which time Nancy decided to lock her door. Mom was seeing red by this point and was standing outside the truck screaming at the top of her lungs. Being in the country and all, sounds tended to carry some distances because there weren't really any other noises to interfere. Charles was working outside the airplane hanger and heard Mom yelling. He took the time to cut a couple of hickory switches that were about an inch thick before heading over to take care of the problem. When he got over to the main road where we were parked, he jerked Nancy out of the truck and threw her in the ditch. He then sat on her and beat her until she was almost unconscious. He was so fat and heavy, that he was literally crushing her and she couldn't breath. When he finally stopped, I thought that he had killed her. Over the next several days as those bruises matured, she was black, blue, green, purple and yellow from her buttocks to her knees. It was horrific to see. I honestly believe to this day that he wanted to kill her.

At the end of the school year, Nancy graduated and enrolled in the University of Tennessee. She wanted to major in agriculture. Nancy really did love farming and all the blood, sweat, and tears that it demanded. It was crucial for Nancy to get away from Charles as she was getting crushed and broken with the constant doses of emotional and physical abuse. Knoxville, Tennessee was over 4 hours away from the ranch. Just far enough that Charles couldn't "drop in."

Meanwhile, Charles decided that Beth needed to attend a college with a Christian environment. Every Sunday morning while we got ready for church, the TV was tuned into the well known preachers of the era. There was Oral Roberts, Jerry Falwell and Rex Humbard. Not only did we "attend" to their sermons on Sunday mornings via the miracle of television; we also sent our tithes and offerings to their ministries. The lot was cast and Oral Roberts was the new college destination for Beth. She was sent off in her Scout that fall to drive the long distance to Tulsa, Oklahoma. At least now she was far enough away that she could not be summoned home on Charles' whim. She settled in quickly and started making friends and seeking some kind of normalcy in life.

Things were about the change dramatically in my life as well. With the mass exodus of my sisters, I was now the lone teenager and the last of the Gilliland girls on the farm. I had gone to school in Alabama through the 8th grade. Many of the kids I went to school with were also the kids we went to church with. I had some good friends that helped me escape from the life on the ranch. With Nancy's departure to college, I no longer had any transportation to get to Alabama. The airport in Athens had long since shut down, so Charles wasn't flying back and forth every day. Mom now had to decide where I would finish my schooling. She decided that the schools in Tennessee were suddenly good enough.

That fall, I got off to a rocky start in 9th grade in Pulaski, Tennessee. Most of the other kids had been in school together their entire lives. In this area, it was expected that people would pretty much stay where they were planted. Families stayed on the same farm, generation after generation and nurtured long and elastic family ties. Not only was I the new kid; I was also an oddity. Having been indoctrinated by Charles for most of my formative years, I could be classified as a religious zealot. To clarify, I carried my Bible to school each day, dressed like a weirdo, didn't hesitate to quote scripture if the opportunity arose and prayed frequently. I was the new circus freak show at the school. The kids called me "Preacher" and I was observed from a distance, but not often interacted with. During my school years in Tennessee, I never fit in or was accepted. Thanks to Charles, there were just too many things stacked against me that made me more of an aberration. He continued to load on all kinds of bizarre rules and regulations. The use of makeup was now strictly forbidden, which was a real shame. Every barn looks better with paint, and I had a good dose of teenaged acne and nothing to camouflage it with.

Getting to school and back home each day was also quite complicated. I had to catch a ride with one of our neighbors on his way to work. He would drive me part way to a little Mom and Pop grocery store, where I would then wait for the county school bus to take me to the Junior High School. In the afternoons, I would ride the bus to the end of the route and walk down the road to a house where a family lived that we barely knew. I would sit outside in all kinds of weather waiting to either catch the Prospect school bus at the end of his route or our neighbor driving home after work. It was anybody's guess how I would get home from school on any given day, or what time I would finally arrive. Looking back, I can say that it really wasn't a very safe means of transport.

chapter 14

1973

Nancy became Charles' next money target when she turned 18 and her money was released from the trust fund. Charles persuaded her to invest in an airplane and a glider, neither of which she would ever see a penny from. Next was a farm, which once again, conveniently bordered his property. The tragic thing about this was that Nancy really did want to farm. The farm that she purchased was in really good shape and she named it "The Cross Ranch". The barn was actually standing upright and the property was completely fenced in, which is a real blessing to anyone who has ever had to string fence. There was also a double-wide trailer on the property which was probably one of the nicest homes in the area. The sale even included a nice tractor, which was soon parked up at that Flying M.

Nancy had some trouble with her courses at the University of Tennessee and dropped out of school. When she first moved back to Prospect, she lived in the trailer on her property. Her independence was short-lived however, because Charles made her move back to the house where he could keep her under his control. She really tried to make it as a farmer but eventually she was unable to keep up with the payments on her farm and the loan rolled over to Charles. This was an addition of 130 acres to the Flying M Ranch.

The absolute worst thing that I ever had to do in my time on that ranch was related to the whole pig fiasco. Several of the cows died from some mysterious illness during the dead heat of the summer. (Pun intended.) Their bloated carcasses were out in the fields where they had up and died. Charles decided that there must be some way to recycle this loss into a profit. It became my designated job to use an ax; (a very dull ax), to chop up the cow carcasses for food for the pigs. Of course this probably violated every health law in existence. I spent hours in the hot summer sun, chopping up these cow carcasses. I learned quickly that it was imperative to avoid hitting the danger zone of the digestive track or I would have the added ordeal of experiencing some of the worst smelling gas fumes ever. By the time the dismemberment was completed, I was covered with little bits of bone, cow hide, and decaying meat while doing this Lizzy Borden-ax-thing all in the middle of hundred degree temperatures. If I close my eyes, I can still hear the sound of the ax chopping into the hairy corpse and feel the little wet pieces of cow hitting my face and arms.

One of the unending jobs on a ranch is bush-hogging. It is the only way to keep a pasture from turning back into a forest. This is done with a tractor and a huge lawnmower attachment thing on the back. We were bush-hogging around the farm years before we were licensed to drive a car. Being several years behind in this task meant that the grass and over-growth was man-high by the time we got started. It would take several days to get a pasture cut, and then it was time to move onto another area. Usually, we were dropped off wherever the tractor might be and picked up at the end of the day. This meant that we were literally cut off from the world, out on the tractor with no way to call for help if something happened.

I was bush-hogging one day way back in Tunnel hollow. I was cutting a pasture that had not been cut in several years and the area was covered with all kinds of tall grass, weeds and tree shoots. At one point, I stopped the tractor to check something on the bush-hog. As I stepped off of the tractor, I narrowly missed stepping on a huge copperhead snake that I had apparently chopped up only minutes before. A few hours later, as I was cutting, I looked down and saw a ginormous rattle snake curled up and striking at the tractor tires as I went by. Instantly, I had both feet up on the steering wheel and was screaming my head off. I had heard stories about snakes getting caught in the tread of the back tractor tires and flipped up on the driver. I was finally able to catch him under the bush hog which made snake fertilizer out of him. Did I mention that I really, really, really hate snakes?

We had one lone survivor from our herd of goats, the rest having fallen prey to hungry predators over the years. This was a billy and he had the misfortune of tangling with a bear trap that someone had set and left out in the woods. It is a miracle that one of us didn't step into the thing. This device was made up of two sets of metal teeth designed to snap closed when a victim stepped in the center. When we found the billy, he was barely alive and the trap was still in place on his front leg with the set chain dragging behind him. Because he was so weak, it didn't take us long to catch and wrestle him to the ground. We brought him into the dining room to try to see what we could do to help him. We never called a vet for any of our animals because it was too expensive. As a result, we would do what we could for the animals and hope for the best. (In all honesty, our experimentation with veterinarian medicine had less than an optimal survival rate. Anything that survived our ministrations was pretty much a miracle.) The poor guy was almost unconscious from panic as we started to attend to his wound. It took a steady hand to release the trap and remove it from his partially amputated leg. His leg was only attached by a few remaining ligaments and tendons which the bolt cutters made short work of. We applied cobwebs (always in ready supply in the house) to the stump of his leg to help curtail any bleeding, wrapped our handiwork up in a makeshift dressing and released him back into the wild. He was appropriately christened "Peg Leg" and he lived for many years, adjusting to life with only three legs and successfully fighting off predators. He was a bit of an inspiration for us. Perhaps that was because he was in the very small percentage of our patients that lived to bahhhh about it.

I had a less than smooth transition from Junior High School to High School. As I started the 10th grade, my reputation for being a freak had preceded me. There were two girls that were a year ahead of me who made it their mission to make my life miserable. They would harass me in the hallways, calling me names and making rude comments. They would corner me as I waited for the school bus after school and ridicule me, making fun of my hair, my clothes, and my beliefs until my bus arrived and I could escape. They got extra creative when they began putting hate letters and notes in my locker. They even made up a petition that was headed "People at Giles County High School that want Ellen Gilliland to leave." On it they had taken turns writing in various names, changing from pen to pencil and blue to black ink. When they ran out of students' names, they started using faculty members' names. I put on a brave face to my tormentors and tucked the hurt way down inside. School was the one place that I was away from Charles, like a temporary sanctuary, but even that place wasn't safe from hate.

chapter 15

1974

After a few years, Charles found the Baptist church in Athens to be too restrictive for him. He became involved in the Pentecostal movement of the 70's, and decided to start his own church in Prospect. They bought one of the abandoned buildings in "downtown" Prospect and named it "The Church of the Living Savior." There was no indoor plumbing and if the urge hit, there was an outhouse in the back. The building had no air-conditioning or source of heat. We bundled up in the winter and used the paddle fans provided by the local funeral home in the summer. They installed a sound system with a microphone and two speakers which were mounted on the *outside* of the building over the door, so that the "word of the Lord could be spread." I am sure that the only thing the people outside of that building ever heard was bad singing and condemnation. Because it was Charles' church, he had complete control. The services could go on for hours until he tired of talking. I was appointed to play the tambourine in an attempt to keep everyone on beat. There was a piano, but it was never tuned and we rarely had anyone who could play it. Most of the hymns were sung to the notes of a harmonica or a saxophone. There were some members that considered themselves to be musically talented and often sang solos. I can testify that not everyone that loves music can sing the tune. The musical renditions at the Church of the Living Savior were more about joyful noises than songs sung on key. With the speakers on the outside of the building, it was a constant source of entertainment for the locals who wisely chose not to attend.

In the Pentecostal church there were some predictable behaviors. Instead of addressing adults at "Miss" or "Mr", they were addressed as "Sister So-and-so" and "Brother So-and-so". And there was the required big hair for the women. Marge Simpson must have gotten her hair inspiration from these women. The higher the hair, the holier the woman (they thought). In order to achieve these monumental bun heights, thousands of bobby pins and cans of hair spray were required. When a sister got "into the spirit", she would commence with lots of flailing of arms and jerking of her body. When the head jerking started, the hair pins would become flying missiles that could impale, causing injury and the need for the laying on of the hands and faith healing. The members would often "swoon" in the spirit, which required the presence of "catchers" at the front of the church to keep them from hitting the pews and floors. Blankets and throws were kept close at hand to prevent any show of immodesty when the ladies collapsed to the floor. Once covered, they would lie there until they recovered enough to return to their seats. It seemed more of a circus atmosphere than a religious meditation.

The next business adventure for the Flying M Ranch was the dairy business. I don't know if Charles really believed they could make money with this or if the idea of really fresh milk overwhelmed any common sense. They purchased a herd of 12 dairy cows from a cattle auction. With the slam of the auctioneer's hammer, we were now in the milking business. At some time in Charles' past, he might have milked a cow or two, but the closest thing we had to any real milking experience was a neighbor. Our first attempts at milking involved taking a bucket and trying to hold the cows still in the corral while fumbling around with their udders. The cows were not impressed and neither was I. I doubt we got enough milk with that first effort to even whiten a cup of coffee. Apparently the only reason that milk cows stand still to be milk is because they are bribed with food and their heads are clamped in place so that running away is no longer an option. It was finally decided that the best place for the new herd would be Nancy's barn. This was a real, honest-to-goodness barn with a rudimentary milking parlor in it. When I use the word, rudimentary, I mean extremely basic tools. There was only access to cold water via a hose; no hot water at all. There were a few hanging light bulbs, but very few outlets in the parlor to plug any equipment in. However, the floor of the "parlor" was concrete, which was a definite step-up from the grass corral.

Dairy cows require milking twice a day. The goal was to get them on a schedule that was about 12 hours apart. There also had to be hay or feed for these ladies to entice them into the milking parlor. We first started out milking all 12 cows by hand. This was slow and tedious work, especially since we really didn't know what we were doing. The milk parlor had 4 stations, which meant that we had three shifts of cows to milk. Diary cows like predictability and routine. Once we established a milking order, they would line up in that order and wait their turn. They would also go to the same stall each time they came into the milking parlor. And they didn't like loud noises or surprises, or they wouldn't let their milk down. (Believe me, this is an actual term and it really does hold true. Piss the cow off and there isn't getting any milk out of her.)

When we first started out, all we had were a couple of milking buckets, some warped milking stools, a milk can in a water-filled chest cooler, and a hose to rinse everything off with. We rigged up a sink that was close to the hose, so that we could wash the equipment. With no hot water, everything had to be sanitized with Clorox. Clorox in direct contact with skin twice a day, 7 days a week, negates any hopes for soft and younger looking hands. Once winter weather set in, cracked hands were a guarantee. The milking parlor was bitterly cold, as there was no insulation and the wind would whip right through the holes in the walls. The water was also freezing cold, when it wasn't solid ice.

We would put the cows in the stalls and then clamped their heads to keep them from changing their minds. Then we would wash their teats off with the (usually freezing) cold water. Now was the time to get up close and personal. We would perch on the milking stool and set the bucket up under their udders. There is a real art to milking a cow by hand. The teat has to be squeezed from the top between the thumb and index finger and then the squeeze is worked down the rest of the teat, forcing the milk out the end. There is no stronger hand shake than that of a dairy farmer. If the cow was a non-kicker, then we would rest our heads against their bellies and go to work. It seemed to take forever before we were finished. It was imperative that every drop of milk be squeezed out of the cow. If we didn't "strip" them at the end of the milking, they would produce less milk. Dairy cows work on the supply and demand principal. The more milk taken, the more milk she will produce, up to a reasonable limit. Also, if not milked dry, the cows could get mastitis, an infection in their udders and a real mess to get cleared up.

Of course, if the cow was a kicker, as was Angel, (don't ask me who named this beast), we had to always keep one hand on the bucket to move fast. Cows kick their back legs in a circular motion. Without warning, the hoof would come up from underneath, knocking over the bucket and whatever precious milk we had obtained, and then would move out at a sharp angle, catching us upside the head. Angel had a great jack hammer effect. Once she knocked us over, she would get in two or three good kicks before we could scurry out of the way.

When our buckets were full, we would pour the milk through a strainer set on top of the milk can. When the milk can was about half full, we had to carefully lift it up and into the water-filled cooler. It was a tricky business to judge when the cans were filled with enough milk that we could still lift them up the 4 feet into the cooler without tipping them over. Then we had to rig up a complicated rope system that would keep the milk cans floating upright in the cold water inside the cooler, as they were still pretty buoyant until filled three-fourths full. A tip-over was a major disaster. The milk can would fill up with water from the cooler and the cooler water would be contaminated with milk. It was also a little tricky pouring the milk through the strainer on the top of the can, as the milk can bobbled around. We were literally trying to hit a moving target. Once the milk cans were full, they would sink on down and sit just fine inside the cooler.

There were all kinds of hazards we had to be on watch for while milking the cows. For example, the bovine fly swatter could be a real tear jerker. Our cows would graze out in the wild blue yonder in between milking times. They would often come in with cocker-burrs in the ends of their tails mixed with dried urine and manure. When cows are contentedly eating, they swish their tails to keep the flies away. That is not a real problem, until one's head is down there in the direct line of the swat. A cow tail face-slap is a real waker-upper early in the morning. Of course, it was worse if the tail was wet.

Another hazard came from their digestive systems. When cows begin eating at one end, they often feel the need to eliminate from the other. There is little warning other than the tail raising that a yellow shower or a green pudding is about to fly. Put some bare feet in the mix, and it's the makings for a real party.

When the cows were done being milked, we would let those girls shuffle out and the next group come in. This pattern continued until everyone was milked and the last drop was poured into the milk can. Then came the fun of cleaning out the dairy parlor. This wasn't so bad in the summer, but in the winter it made a cold place even colder. All of the equipment had to be washed and sanitized in the cold, cold water and Clorox. Then the dairy room had to be hosed out, or the flies would be unbearable. We kept the area decorated with dangling spirals of yellow fly paper, but they could only hold so many of the unending population. The entire process would take a couple of hours twice a day. We were a "Grade C" barn, which meant that our milk could only be sold for cheese. The dairy guy would come twice a week, picking up the full milk cans and leaving empty ones for us to fill.

Mom absolutely loved the idea of having fresh milk. She would pour it into glass jars and keep it in the fridge. When we went to get it out, there would be about 3 inches of cream on the top. She then got the bright idea of making butter. This involved a butter churn and lots of elbow grease. After what seemed like hours of churning the cream, we had produced about 2 tablespoons of butter. It wasn't even enough to put a shine on the morning toast.

An unpleasant reality was that whatever the cows ate had a direct impact on the flavor of their milk. A real genuine dairy farm controls the diet of the herd 24/7. On the Flying M Ranch, that was not the case. Our cows would wander out into the pasture and graze in between milkings. On occasion, they would get hold of green onions. There is nothing grosser than pouring a big glass of milk and taking that first big swig only to have every taste bud rise up in protest at the disgusting flavor of green onion milk. As a result of this trauma, I still have to sniff my milk before I can drink it, even though it comes sealed from the grocery store. Old habits die hard.

After many months, we got upgraded to electric milkers, which were really nice because they were self-contained units. If the cow (Angel, specifically) knocked them over, the milk didn't spill out. Also, we could milk a couple of cows at the same time, which was a vast improvement over hand milking. Of course, things would still go wrong with the equipment, but this cut milking time in half.

There are some special milk barn memories. One day, Nancy and I were up at the barn milking the cows. Nancy said that she didn't think that the electric fence was working around the pasture outside. Somehow she talked me into going out and "testing" it. Being a dumbbell, I dutifully went out and grabbed hold of the fence. It charged up my batteries for sure. What made me really mad was that I could hear her laughing all the way outside of the barn.

When Nancy and I were milking cows, we had to do the evening milking right before church on Sunday and Wednesday nights. The milk barn was on Nancy's farm that was up off of the main road. We would come directly to church with our shoes covered with manure, our tattered clothes covered with sweat; smelling like the barnyard and worse. One night when we got to the service late, Charles called me over to him. He told me to go back to the house and let Brock, the-German Shepherd-pet-killer, loose. I was tired, dirty and frustrated because Charles was just at the house before church and only had to drive down the hill and unclip Brock's chain. Needless to say, I was a little perturbed. But I was also smart enough to know not to push his buttons. So I went out of the church to do his bidding. He came running after me and slammed me up against the car, hitting me in my face, giving me a bloody nose. He said that I had slammed the church door when I went out. Let's face it; the church doors were old, misshapen and didn't close right anyway. They had to be slammed to get them to close. He then made me go back into the church and apologize with my nose bleeding to the entire congregation for slamming the door. When I went back out, I was extra careful closing the door this time, but he still came after me, saying I had slammed the door again. I got to do a second take on the humble apology and when I exited that time, I didn't even try to close the darned door. It was a no win situation.

As my sixteenth birthday approached, Charles found an International Scout for sale and it was purchased with my trust fund money with no input from me. To make it worse, this vehicle was a convertible. Putting the roof down really wasn't an option, as it no longer folded, having weathered too long in the upright position. All the fabric roof did was make this vehicle about 10 degrees colder in the winter. This car was a standard shift, as were all of the vehicles on the ranch. On my 16th birthday, Mom and I drove about 40 minutes to the closest DMV. It was the first time that I had ever driven anywhere that actually had stoplights. Miraculously I passed on my first try. I was the proud holder of a colored piece of paper issued by the great state of Tennessee that said I was legal to drive. No ID picture or lamination process involved. And I was now the new driver for the ranch and for the church bus route.

Charles required us to do all of the repairs on our cars. One afternoon I was working on my Scout. I had it parked on top of the hill next to the carport. It was idling in neutral, as I was adjusting the carburetor. Mom yelled from the house that I had a phone call. I left the car running, with the parking brake on and went in to answer the phone. While talking on the phone, I heard Mom screaming at the top of her lungs. Lo and behold, the Scout had started rolling backwards down the hill. It was picking up good speed as it raced down the incline. Finally, it hit a bump at the bottom of the hill, jumped the sorry excuse for a fence, bounced off of the railroad track and landed sideways in the gully that ran along the track. The frame on the car was bent and it was history. I never shed a tear. Nothing like a car suicide to liven things up.

A few days later, Charles informed me that we were going to Nashville to buy another car for me. This time the unauthorized-vehicle-purchased-with-my-trust-fund-money was an International Travelall. This one of those hideous oversized station wagons, in an unsightly turquoise hue. It was so big, that I had to look through the steering wheel just to see over the dashboard. Charles had chosen this particular vehicle because I would be able to pick up more people on his church route. Not only was this car a piece of junk; at age 16, it was a complete embarrassment to drive.

I was now able to drive myself to school, but Charles would only let me drive as far as the Mom and Pop store. I had to leave my car parked there and catch the school bus the rest of the way. This lasted only until Charles realized that I could do errands for them in town after school. Other kids got notes about important stuff, like doctors' appointments and such. My notes were about going by the parts store or the

Co-Op on the way home to pick up supplies for the ranch.

The church bus route now became my responsibility. This was two round trips on Sunday and one on Wednesday evenings. I spent hours on Sundays and Wednesdays driving around the back roads alone, stopping at houses to see if anyone wanted a ride to church. This might have been the only contact that some of those people had all week with the outside world. It led to an interesting congregational mix.

Charles continued to make up rules so ridiculous that it was only a matter of time until we broke them. One of his rules was that I was not to drive my station wagon over 35 miles an hour. That was crazy slow, even by country standards. One evening a group of us teenagers played car tag on the back roads. We were having a good time and not hurting anyone. I did exceed the 35 MPH limit, speeding up to 50 at one point. One of the girls in the group ratted me out to Charles. Unfortunately, I was blissfully unaware of the storm that was brewing. When I got home Sunday night after driving the bus route, he was waiting for me in the kitchen. Mom was not at home and Nancy was in the back den. He grabbed me and started yelling. When I looked into his face, I swear that his eyes were yellow and glowing. He threw me on the floor, pulled up my skirt and beat me with his belt. I was bruised from my waist to my knees. Mom later made him apologize for pulling up my skirt, but not for the beating. I could barely walk and sitting down was agony. It took weeks for the bruises to fade.

Nancy had a legendary temper and being hard headed, I wasn't one to back down from her moods. A smarter person would have just given her a wide berth and left her alone. Apparently, I just wasn't all that smart. One day we got into a yelling match. I can't even remember what it was about. It really didn't matter because we were both spoiling for a fight. It was a Sunday afternoon and we were very limited on what we were allowed to do on "the day of rest". Nancy made a smart comment and I topped it off. She flew into my bedroom and we got into the knock-down-drag-out fight of our lives. I had my hair rolled up on a set of those sadistic electric rollers. They were the ones that had the hard plastic spikes on them that would get so tangled up in the hair that cutting them out seemed the only option for removal. We took a few swings at each other and then we started with the hair pulling. Nancy hated to have her hair pulled and I was well aware of that fact. I yanked out a good hand-full before she started beating me about the head with her fists. Of course, what she was actually doing was hammering those plastic spikes into my scalp. By the end of the fight, she had a few bald spots and I was sporting a bloody nose and had puncture wounds all over my head from the curler spikes. This was the last of our physical fights because we both came to the realization that there really were no winners in altercations like this.

One day, out of the blue, Charles decreed that frogs were unclean animals. He quoted some random scripture verse to back up his decision. It was just another example of his Christian malpractice. I am sure that it had more to do with the fact that he hated Nancy, than in any real conviction in Charles' dark soul. Nancy had been collecting frogs since she was a little girl in Pennsylvania. She had an amazing variety of ceramic, glass, and metal frogs in all shapes and sizes. Each one had sentimental value to her. But Charles had made his announcement and expected immediate removal of the unclean objects from his kingdom. Nancy tearfully packed up her collection and the two of us drove out to the single lane bridge. There we gave each of them a tearful send off into a watery grave. Mom was unaware until after the "unclean frogs" were disposed of that Charles' banishment affected her also. While packing up the frogs, Nancy had included a frog shaped doorstop that Mom's deceased brother had made. It had great sentimental value to her. Mom was furious about the loss of her special frog when she realized it had been sent to the bottom of the river. But what could she say? If the big man said something was unclean, then it shouldn't really matter who it belonged to, right?

There was never a dull or normal day on the Flying M Ranch. One afternoon Nancy got back from town with a tractor tire on the back of one of the flatbed trucks. (This was a big rear-wheel tractor tire.)

She had taken it into town to get it patched. She shoved it off the back of the truck, with the expectation that it would take a few bounces and fall over. However, the Law of Physics would prove her wrong. The tire made a prefect landing on the tread and took off rolling down the hill, straight for a newly painted airplane that was sitting on the runway. I watched in stupefied horror as Nancy ran down the hill trying to tackle the speeding object multiple times as it raced towards the plane. Miraculously, it turned at the last millisecond and hit the corner of the burned-out trailer where Charles stored parts. He pitched a fit about the corner of the trailer getting banged up. Imagine what would have happened if it had destroyed the plane.

chapter 16

1975

Feeding the animals was a huge financial concern each year. We depended on hay, but if the weather did not cooperate, then there would not be enough harvested for the winter. One alternative was the cookie factory in Pulaski. Farmers could get scoops of rejected cookies dropped into their truck beds on Saturday mornings for free. Feeding the cookies to animals was one thing. Our frugal mom had other ideas. She had us sort through the cookies on the back of the pickup. (Please note that these cookies were the rejected cookies from the cookie plant for legitimate cookie rejection reasons.) Any that weren't too broken or crushed were placed into trash bags in big trashcans. We would eat these rejects for months and share them with company. The rest of the cookies got used for their intended purpose which was to feed the cows, horses, and pigs.

During the winter, I was required to come home directly from school and haul hay to feed cows in three different fields, by myself. This would take me hours, and the bales of hay weighed more than I did. I would be white with cold by the time I finished. Even if there was an activity after school, I had to make the 30 minute trip home first and feed all of the cows, and then go back to school. Mom, of course, would be down in the hanger slaving away on whatever airplane project they had going. Charles would be in the house, lying in front of the heat vent staying toasty warm. The thinking job seemed to have much better perks than the grunt jobs that I always seemed to get.

There wasn't much for a teenager to do in Prospect, and Charles pretty much nixed anything that sounded like fun. Of course, any fun activities had to be scheduled after we had finished all of our work and chores. We were sometimes allowed to go to the roller skating rink in Ardmore, a little town about 20 minutes away. The skating rink was a primitive wood structure that had plywood window flaps that were propped open during the warm weather, and left closed during the cold. It wasn't a very big rink. By the time we were getting our "groove thing on", it was time to make the turn at the end. We didn't mind, though, as it was the only place to hang out with other kids our age. The rink had a couple of speakers set up in the corners and the music was turned up loud, so we didn't pay attention to the peeling paint or uneven floors. The uneven floors just made staying upright on our skates all the more challenging. Some of the kids got pretty creative with their skating techniques. Kung Fu Fighting was a hit song, and there were many accidents while attempting our kung fu kicks and trying to stay balanced on our skates.

Whenever we went out to roller-skate, Charles' dictates made our fashion options very limited. We could either wear a long skirt, known as Maxi dresses in the 70's, or we could wear pants with the mandatory skirt over top. It was a little tricky skating in a skirt that went to the floor. One time that I did the pants / skirt combination, and shed the skirt when we got to the roller rink. One of the kids snitched on me to Charles. I was the recipient of another beating that left a montage of bruises on my body. It was always a dilemma trying to weigh the cost before breaking the dress code. Sometimes it just seemed worth the risk to be able to look like a normal teenager for a few hours.

Meanwhile, back in Tulsa at Oral Roberts University, Beth had met someone special. His name was Mike and he was a big man on campus. She was in love and they wanted to get married. Charles was enraged because he had picked out some pansy guy from Athens for her to marry. Beth held firm, and Mom and Charles disowned her. When Beth realized the inevitable, she used part of her trust money to pay off her car and her next semester's tuition at school. When Mom and Charles found out, they were furious. They wiped out her checking account, all of her savings, and kept her monthly social security checks.

They turned their backs on her, leaving her stranded at college with no financial or emotional support. It was a deliberate and cruel thing to do. To make matters worse, they wrote horrible letters to her stating what a terrible person she was and made Nancy and I sign them. All of the things in her bedroom were boxed up and sent to her, cash-on-delivery. Beth had no idea what was in the boxes, so she had to pay the postage, only to open them up to find worthless junk. She went ahead and married Mike with Grandma Jones in attendance for moral and emotional support. Back in Prospect, Charles bought Mom a state-of-the-art microwave oven as compensation for missing her daughter's wedding. I am sure that in reality it was Mom's money that paid for the bribe.

Mom finally came to the realization that if Nancy stayed on the ranch, it was only a matter of time before Charles killed her emotionally and literally. Mom and Charles decided that she would attend the Bible Institute at Jerry Falwell's college. When Nancy applied to the school, Mom and Charles told me to also fill out an application for the academy. I was excited about the prospect of escaping from Charles for my senior of high school and began to watch the mail each day to see if my prayers would be answered. When my letter of acceptance arrived, I made the mistake of telling Charles that God had shown me what His will was. I was to attend the academy, because the acceptance letter was an answer to my prayers. Charles whipped around and proclaimed that

God would not talk to me, but would tell him what I was to do. That was an epiphany for me and a defining moment in my life. I walked into the house, looked my mother in the eye, and told her that Jesus Christ had died so that I didn't need a high priest or a step-father to tell me what to do. Even though I was not allowed to attend the academy, I was a wiser person spiritually and became determined to escape from the clutches of Charles in my own due time.

I began to examine what kind of person Charles was and if people really wanted to be associated with his god. The answer was crystal clear to me. The god that he preached about was a god that judged people on their outward appearance and ruled that no one was ever good enough to be accepted. My Bible spoke of a God that loved us so much that He sent His only begotten Son to die for us and He welcomed everyone, including prostitutes, murderers and more. I had a revelation and decided that the best testimony a person could have was to walk the life and be a living example of God's love. Religion is something that is caught, not taught. I stopped turning people off by talking about religion non-stop. Charles sensed the change in me. He would spy on me, stopping by my high school and checking inside my car to see if I had taken my Bible with me. After I got in trouble for that offense, I started taking it into school and putting it in my locker.

Meanwhile, Nancy was put on a bus to Lynchburg, Virginia, where she was to start school. In time, Nancy began to recover emotionally and even joined one of the choruses from the college that traveled around the country singing and sharing their testimonies. She worked in the kitchen at the school to help pay for her tuition. She began to see what normal could be like.

There was a young couple that rented a house from Mom and Charles. They were newlyweds with a baby girl. One night, to my surprise, they invited me over to their house after church. I said that was fine, as long as they had Charles' approval. Charles told them it was okay, but I had to run the bus route first and take everyone home. After I finished the circuit, I drove over to their house. We were sitting around their kitchen table, talking with the screen door and windows open to let in a breeze. We heard a car pull up front and went outside to see who it was. It was Mom and Charles. Mom got out of the car, screaming at me at the top of her lungs. Apparently, Charles didn't tell her that he had given me permission to go to the couple's house after finishing the church route. She freaked out because I wasn't home when I was supposed to be. The next thing I knew, she was coming at me with a broom and was bashing me over the head with it. Instinctively, I tried to grab it to protect myself, while attempting to figure out why she was flipping out on me. This ticked Charles off and he then got in on the beating. When it was all over, he said that I should have come by the house after I had completed the bus route to let them know I was finished. It became very apparent to me that socializing just wasn't worth the literal headaches.

As I started my senior year in high school, the Travel-all was no longer reliable. It was breaking down on a regular basis with ailments so problematic that not even the great Charles Meagher could remedy them. Charles was already working hard to convince me to buy a farm when my trust fund money was released. I had watched my sisters lose everything to this man and walk away with hardly the clothes on their backs. When Charles began his campaign to enlarge the Flying M Ranch, thanks to my investment, I was prepared. I told him that the only investment I was going to make would be a fast car to get as far away as possible from the Flying M Ranch. And the only part of the Flying M Ranch I wanted was the reflection of it in my rearview mirror as I drove away. And that is just what I did.

Because I had pointblank refused to consider the purchasing of property to benefit the Flying M Ranch, I finally got to pick out the car I wanted. My favorite TV show was the Rockford Files. I knew that there was no hotter car than the Pontiac Firebird. Mom and I went to the big city of Huntsville, Alabama to look at cars. In one showroom, there was a white Firebird and a red Trans-Am. When we got home, Charles asked Mom which car I was going to get, and she said the red Trans-Am of course. What a delight it was to get into that car and drive it home. I couldn't believe it was really mine. One of the guys from Prospect had gone with us and did the maiden voyage home with me. I was so excited. Charles waited until I got home to rain on my parade. He berated me for driving the car too fast. He said that the engine had to be broken in and I was not to drive it over 45 miles per hour for the first 5,000 miles. (Who was he kidding?) I now had my fast car to make my get away.

It was September of my senior year and out of the blue, I drove up in a brand new fire-engine red 1975 Pontiac Trans Am to school. I cannot begin to explain how this changed my status in high school. The first day I drove it, we had class elections for class officers. Unbelievably, I was elected to be Vice-President of our Senior Class. These positions were more of a popularity contest and not so much about job qualifications. Without a doubt, if I had driven my red Trans Am to school one day later, my fate would have been different. This car, this acceptance (in a small way) by my peers, made a huge difference in my self esteem and began to give me some self confidence. It is such a hard thing to be 16 years old and trying to find somewhere to fit in.

The next incredible thing that happened to me that fall was that I met someone special. His name was Ryan and we were introduced by a common friend. He was a senior at Prospect High School and president of his senior class (of 12 students). He played basketball and was an all around good guy. Ryan was completely different from the guys that I knew from school. He was even brave enough to come up to the house to meet Charles and ask him if we could go out on a date. Surprisingly, Charles said yes. We double dated with friends and played Putt Putt golf. When he kissed me goodnight (this was my very first kiss) I was sunk. Here was a guy who cared enough to put up with Charles so that we could date. During our romance, Charles would come up with all kinds of ridiculous conditions and rules to discourage him. Charles dictated how long his hair could be and he was required to attend our church services. If he failed to meet these stipulations and many others, then we weren't allowed to date. Ryan was willing to jump through all Charles' crazy hoops. This guy just fixed something in my heart.

I don't think that Ryan had any idea of what kind of impact he had on my life. When I first met him, I was the last slave left on the ranch. Beth had left home, gone to college and gotten married. Nancy was still at school in Virginia. All of the chores and grunt work were now my responsibility. I had no one left that I could talk to, because the local kids would play Judas on me in a heartbeat. I was to the point where I was actually contemplating suicide. It was a dark time in my life. I had the perfect spot picked out along the church route where it would only take a slight turn of the wheel, and it would be over. I felt hopeless and there seemed to be no escape from the nightmare that I was living. Being the last one left at home, every aspect of my life was under constant scrutiny by Charles. The pressure never let up.

Dating options were very limited in this small community. The one main date option was to go to the drive-in movie in Pulaski. Dating at the drive-in had many challenges. The speakers never seemed to work right, it was hard to see through the windshield, and there were lots of eyes watching all around us. In the summer, it was hot and in the winter it was cold. Our other date option was to sit on the front porch of the house during the nice weather (with Mom and Charles upstairs) or watch TV in the den when it got chilly. Somehow we made it work, though.

We continued to date throughout our senior year. Ryan gave me hope that there was something beyond that ranch and my sadistic stepfather. His family was normal and he had a good home life. I can't imagine what his parents thought about me or my so-called family. The beginnings of self-confidence started to bloom and I began to realize that Charles was only a man, and not God's right hand, as he seemed to believe. I began to hope for what tomorrow might bring, and made plans for college. As I prepared to go off to college, we began to talk about a long term commitment.

Sometimes the hay crop was not bountiful enough to feed cows for the entire winter due to lack of rain, too much rain, or failure to get the hay in for some reason. During these times we would have to buy hay from other farmers. This meant that we had to take the truck to another farm and load the hay from their hayloft, stack it onto the truck, drive it to one of our barns, and unload it. One day, Charles sent me and three teenaged guys to pick up a load of hay. We went in a big Marine truck that Charles had bought off of someone. The deal was that we could either do it in two smaller runs, or try to get all of the hay on the truck in one load. I had a date with my guy that night and wanted to get it over with. Things went pretty well as we loaded up the truck. We meticulously stacked the bales and then secured them with several ropes. This particular truck had welded tie holds along the sides. We were careful to pull the ropes tight and fasten them through the tie holds. All was well until we made a turn off the main highway and one of the welded holds broke off the truck. It was like watching a spring-loaded rocket take off. The rope completely unwrapped, and the bales started falling like a house of cards. There were hay bales all over the road. Once a hay bale bounces around on asphalt, it is never a nice rectangle again. There was the initial shock, and then being teenagers, the inevitable embarrassment.

There is nothing on earth that can run as fast as a rumor in a small town. The gossip of our hay bale dilemma arrived home way before we did. We scrambled to get the hay back on the truck, but since the bales were now more round than rectangular, they didn't stack very well. It was a long trip home at 15 miles per hour, with frequent stops to pick up the bales as they rolled off. By the time we got home, all three of the guys were laying spread eagle on top of the hay in an effort to try to hold the bales on the truck. When we got to the bridge over the creek, we lost about ½ of the load again. When we finally got out to Shoney's barn to unload it, the sun was setting. I pulled in close to the barn, and predictably, the truck got stuck in the muck. I had to walk all the way back to the house to get Charles to come and get the truck out of the ooze. I don't know how many hours this adventure lasted but I know the emotional scars are still there. Every time I pass a truck loaded down with hay bales, my arm pits get all sweaty.

Now there is nothing any more entertaining and exciting in the country than chasing critters. One hot summer day, Nancy and I, along with a couple of teenagers, were back in one of the hollows. When we were going through a gate on a farm, we spotted a family of skunks. Now we had enough smarts to know to avoid the mamma skunk. However, the babies were so cute and we really didn't think that they were born equipped to spray. So we commenced trying to catch a baby skunk. We didn't chase very long, because believe me, baby skunks *are* equipped to spray. The other kids took a direct hit. It was a long ride home in the back of the Scout with no air conditioning. Skunk spray will definitely bring a tear to one's eye and limit the intake of deep breaths.

One night, Ryan, Nancy, and I took a drive over the Hanahward Bridge. This rickety wooded bridge was reported to be of historical significance and also just happened to be condemned. The actual roadbed of the bridge was made of wooden slats that made this weird noise as we drove over them. It was a freaky and scary place to be, especially at night. It was also supposedly haunted (of course) by a young girl whom the old timers said jumped to her death from the bridge. As we started to drive across this precarious structure, we spotted a possum in the middle. We were overcome with an irresistible urge to test the theory that possums will always play possum when spotlighted with a flashlight. We stopped the car in the middle of the condemned bridge and put the lights on the ugly critter. Mr. Possum did not lie down and play dead. He scurried to the edge and jumped off the bridge into the river below. He decided that his odds were better with the river than with mankind.

chapter 17

1976

I graduated from high school on a Saturday morning and left for college the very next day. Beth and her new husband, Mike, came home for my high school graduation. It was their first trip home since their wedding (that we weren't allowed to attend.) They were pretty nervous about the entire thing, but all-in-all, things seemed to go pretty well. Perhaps Charles had given up on his arranged marriage plans for Beth, or maybe he still had hope that things would not work out.

Sunday morning, less than 24 hours after receiving my high school diploma, I was put into my car with most of my worldly belongings, given some really old maps and bad directions, and sent off into the wild blue yonder for a faraway place called Greenville, South Carolina. With Beth at Oral Robert's University in Oklahoma and Nancy at Jerry Falwell's Liberty College in Virginia, the last choice in religious colleges was Bob Jones University. I got lost multiple times along the way and the trip took much longer than it should have. I had absolutely no idea where I was going. One lady who was trying to help me with directions asked me where in the world I had gotten the map I was using, because half of the roads listed were no longer there. Charles did not believe in driving the interstate, so I was on back roads for the entire journey. By some miracle, I finally arrived in Greenville and got lost again in the city trying to find the college. I finally located the campus and after circling the fenced-in grounds several times, found my dormitory. My roommates were both gone for the weekend, so I had to unpack my entire car by myself, lugging everything up the steps to the second floor. Back home in Prospect, Mom was anxiously awaiting for my phone call to let her know that I had arrived safe and sound. But alas, they had left the phone off of the hook after church, and all I got was a busy signal when I tried to call.

Being completely clueless, I registered for my first summer semester in college with profound optimism. I signed up for 3 classes – History of Civilization, English 101 and Tennis. Tennis sounded like an easy A, but at Bob Jones University, PE classes had skills tests as well as written tests to ensure competency. This month of classes almost killed me. I was reading two chapters a night in history with tests almost everyday. Each week I was painfully typing out a term paper on my electric typewriter for English. If there were four misspelled words in the paper, it was an automatic F. (Misspelled words were easy to make and hard to correct on the old typewriters.) And last, but not least, I was trying to learn the ins and outs of tennis. I somehow passed all three of my courses and then enrolled for the second summer semester, signing up for only two courses this time. In August, I headed home for a few weeks before resuming my college education in Greenville for the fall semester.

I had learned many things during my accelerated college experience. I began to realize that there was a huge world out there beyond the boundaries of Giles County Tennessee. Ryan and I were still an item, but I knew without a doubt that Tennessee was the last place I wanted to be. He, on the other hand, had a normal family and didn't want to live anywhere else. We continued to write each other faithfully.

That fall semester, the dorm room I was sharing with four other girls, was the size of a very small bedroom. We had a double bunk on one side of the room and a triple bunk on the other side. I slept on the top of the triple, which was so close to the ceiling that when I rolled over at night, my elbows scraped the plaster. It was an interesting experience of trying to achieve some kind of harmony with all of that estrogen in one small space. People who meet me now cannot believe that I was not immediately expelled from Bob Jones. The school is well known for having massive amounts of rules, regulations, and religious constraints for their students with zero tolerance. However, I had lived with outrageous rules and restrictions for the last 12 years of my life. At BJU, the rules didn't change on someone's whim or mood, which actually made life much improved for me.

When I went home for Christmas break, the planned project for our holiday was to put a roof on a shed in the backyard by the swimming pool to park my TransAm in while I was at college. (This was, of course, funded by money taken from my trust fund.) But first on Mom's to-do list was for Nancy and me to move a railroad tie. This was a creosote-coated monster that weighed about 200 pounds. Nancy dropped her end first, which cause the thing to twist and smash my right hand. Mom and Charles were deep into faith healing, so going to the doctor or the emergency room for treatment wasn't an option. I broke at least two or three bones in my right hand and was in excruciating pain. It was swollen to three times its normal size and I was unable to move my fingers. I bandaged it the best I could with a piece of wood and an ace bandage. The pain was intense and kept me awake all night. But on the Flying M Ranch, injuries were not allowed to slow down a job, and neither would the weather.

The next day found Nancy and me perched on the roof of the shed in an ice storm, trying to keep from sliding off. I was unsuccessfully trying to hammer nails into the shingles with my left hand, while cradling my injured right hand close to my body. Charles kept bellowing at me because I kept missing the nails. An interesting side note is that my car never even made it inside this shed that I had paid for. They filled it up with junk.

chapter 18

1977

During the spring of my first year in college, I started praying about where I was going to spend my summer. I knew that if I went back home, I would never escape from Tennessee or Charles. I did an interview and got offered a job at a camp as a lifeguard and counselor. Mom and Charles were both on the phone when I told them about my summer employment. Charles was enraged. He accused me of being rebellious and disobedient. He ranted and raved that God would always tell him what I was supposed to do. He again said that God would not talk to me. I stuck to my guns, and told them that I had prayed about it and God had opened up this door. That didn't go over well at all. Charles yelled into the phone that if I took the summer job then I was disowned and was to never come home again. Mom said that she supported his decision. I told them that I was sorry, but I was taking the job. I was 18 years old.

After slamming down the phone on me, Mom and Charles immediately called the Dean of Women at the college and told her that I was rebellious and disobedient and demanded that I be kicked out of the school. After explaining the situation to my dormitory supervisor, the college said they would support me. The first thing I did the next morning was to call my bank in Tennessee where I had a joint checking account with my mother. I had her name removed from the account, because the money in the account belonged to me. When Charles and Mom had disowned Beth, they closed out her checking account and took what was left of her trust fund, along with her monthly social security checks, leaving her with nothing. I was determined that they weren't going to do the same thing to me. I can only imagine how enraged Charles was when he realized that I had literally closed the door to the vault.

The next thing on my list to finding the real me was to get my waist length hair cut short into the popular Dorothy Hamill wedge. I loved it and felt like a new person. I also began going by my middle name. I was creating a new identity and I liked the person that I was becoming. I was starting to live my life for the very first time.

The only thing that was left on the ranch that I really wanted was my red Trans Am. I began to investigate different possibilities of how to get it without bloodshed. Should I hire a police officer to go up there with me and protect me? Should I just go up and take it when they weren't home? It was a real dilemma. Late in the spring semester, I was walking across campus on my way back to my dorm room when I heard my mother call my name. I knew it was her, but when I stopped and looked around, I didn't see anyone. When I walked into my dorm, the desk monitor told me that someone had dropped off some keys for me at the desk. She held up my car keys. When I walked out the back of my dorm, there was my car with every item from my bedroom crammed into the car. I was so ecstatic! Not only did I get my car, but it was delivered to Greenville for me with all of my belongings. Mom would later tell me that they dropped my car off on their way to Virginia for Nancy's graduation from the Bible Institute. She said that when she saw me walking across campus, she called my name. Charles told her to shut-up and they hustled off campus. It would be several months before I would see my mom again. After my disowning, I faithfully sent a card or letter to my mom every week. They were all returned to me unopened with "return to sender" written across the front of the envelope. Our cyclic mail must have driven the post office staff crazy.

I had to get special permission to keep my car on campus because only seniors were allowed to have cars, and I wasn't allowed to drive it. I also had all of my stuff from home. It was now time to start my life. When school let out for the summer, I rented a room from a widowed lady. She usually had a couple of college girls staying there at any given time. It was a safe place and even though the accommodations weren't fancy, they were good enough for temporary.

She did have a problematic green thumb, however. The entire main floor of her house was filled with plants that were growing up and around everything. They would caress me when I would walked by. It was like a science fiction movie that had lots of possibilities for a bad ending.

I began my new job at the camp, which was exhausting mentally as well as physically. Campers arrived bright and early every Monday and they stayed through Saturday morning. We would then drive back to town, do our wash at the Laundromat, attend church on Sunday and head back to camp bright and early on Monday to do it all over again. I started gaining some self-confidence that summer. It was fun to work with the kids and see them try new things. Many of the campers were dealing with their own life challenges.

One of my jobs was being the girls' lifeguard. At this particular camp, boys and girls were not allowed to swim together. The kids had to pass a swim test in order to be allowed to venture out to a floating raft in the middle of the lake. One day I was swimming with a group of girls out to the raft. For some reason, one of the girls got panicked and started to go under. I got behind her and pushed her to safety. She was fine, but this experience made me realize the seriousness of my job and that there could be deadly consequences if I didn't do it correctly. It was one of those defining moments of realizing that life isn't a dress rehearsal and people's lives depended on me giving my best at all times.

The only real connection that I had left in Tennessee was my guy. By taking the camp job in South Carolina, I had pretty much sealed our fate. At the end of the summer, Ryan drove out to see me. By this time, I had decided that there was no future for us. I was not very kind to him. I gave him his senior ring back and told him that I wanted to break up. To this day, I feel terrible about how I handled this. He still wanted to spend some time together, but my heart wasn't in our relationship any longer. I don't think that either of us enjoyed our last day together. I am ashamed of how I treated this person who had literally saved my life, but I knew that our love was not the kind that would last a lifetime.

Ryan would move on with life and so would I. When I found my sweet prince and we got engaged, Mom put the announcement in the local paper in Tennessee. Ironically, my old beau's wedding announcement was on the same page.

I spent that Christmas alone in my rented room off campus in Greenville. I drove up to Michigan for New Years to spend the last of the holidays with one of my college buddies. Her family was fabulous at making me feel welcome. I got to experience snowmobiling and cross country skiing for the first time and had a blast.

chapter 19

1978

Nancy graduated from the Bible Institute when she was 24 years old. While in school, she had really grown as an individual and a Christian. She had even started to gain a little self confidence. When she moved back to Tennessee, she made attempts to be independent and got a job in a nearby city working at a stock barn. Mom and Charles went by the stockyard to spy on her and caught her without her skirt over her pants. There was hell to pay for this infraction. Nancy seemed unable to resist the lure of the farm and the need to have her parents' love and approval. Things continued to get progressively worse. She was on the ranch by herself, as Beth was married in Tulsa and I was off at college and had been disowned.

Nancy finally reached her breaking point. One night, in the spring on Good Friday, she packed up her car in the middle of the night and left for Beth's house in Tulsa. She stopped only long enough to call Beth to tell her that she was on her way. When Nancy arrived, she was so emotionally tattered, that she couldn't even make a decision about what she wanted to drink. It would take a long time for her to even begin to function normally again.

I was estranged from my mom until Christmas of 1978. Nancy flew to Greenville and the two of us drove to Tennessee for the holidays. We planned our trip carefully so that we would only be under Charles' roof for a matter of hours. Mom was glad to have us home, even for a short time. We were trying to have a relationship with her, which impaired by the constant presence of Charles.

chapter 20

1979

Life would move on for me. There was college and nursing school, roommates and romance. I met the love of my life and we began talking about marriage. I had prayed for this man for many years, never knowing who or where he was. I knew that if he was truly the one for me, then nothing would prevent us from getting married. His name was Greg and he was even willing to drive to Tennessee to meet Mom and Charles and to ask for my hand in marriage. What an adventure this turned out to be.

I tried to prepare Greg for Prospect, the Flying M Ranch and Charles, but I think he really thought I was exaggerating. In reality, I probably was holding back a little to keep from scaring him off. Greg was a city boy with no exposure to country things at all. We headed off in the early spring of 1979 to Tennessee. When we arrived at the farm, Mom and Charles were going to a church meeting. We felt obligated to tag along. I don't think Greg had ever experienced anything quite like that, having been raised a Baptist and all. On the way home after the church experience, Mom suddenly stopped the car and told me to get out to pick up a dead rabbit on the road. I almost died of embarrassment and told her that under no circumstances was I putting the dead rabbit in the back of the car with us. She finally relented and drove on. I don't think Greg totally comprehended the situation until I explained it after we were married.

Finally came the time for Greg to speak with Charles about our plans to marry. This totally inflated Charles' ego and he cockadoodled about like he was the big cheese. The end result was that Charles said that he would need to pray about this matter to see what "God's Will" was and would get back to Greg. We headed back to Greenville with no answer. After 2 long weeks, Charles finally called Greg and told him that God was neutral on our marriage because the rapture was going to happen on July 7th of that year, so the wedding, planned for November would never take place. We took that as a yes and ran with it.

When July 7th came and went with no trumpet call or rapture, Charles began to rethink his position. That September, Greg and I traveled back to Prospect with my prospective in-laws for the "meeting" of the families. The first thing Charles said when we got out of the car after an 8 hour drive was that it was a sin for a woman to wear clothing that pertaineth to a man, because I was wearing blue jeans. Not a great impression for my future family. Things pretty much went south from there. Charles was determined to prove that he was king of the castle and the rest of us were not impressed with the kingdom. My future mother-in-law remarked after looking around the house, that the only thing it really needed was a match, and she was right. The trip was cut short by faking a family emergency back in Greenville and we escaped back to civilization. The good thing was that Greg's family realized that Charles was a dangerously fanatical man and certifiably insane.

As November grew near, I had many things going on in my life. I was graduating from nursing school, in charge of the pinning ceremony for said graduation, planning our wedding, and trying to find a job. In the midst of these events, I got a letter from Charles that said I was rebellious and must immediately come home to ask for their forgiveness in person, so that they could give their blessing on our wedding. There was no doubt in any of our minds that if I went back to Tennessee alone, I would never be heard from again. It was absolutely not going to happen.

Our church pastor was a man that only saw things in black and white. He had stated many times that he would never marry someone who did not have their parents' blessing. My future father-in-law was a deacon at the church, and was well liked and respected. He went to the pastor and explained the situation and how unstable Charles was. Even with these facts, the pastor was still reluctant to perform the ceremony.

I was sure that Charles would not let Mom come to the wedding by herself and we for sure did not want him to be there. Two days before the wedding, I got a 3x5 index card in the mail that had a flight number, date and arrival time on it. That was it. No name or other information. I had to assume it was from Mom. We went to the airport on the afternoon of our wedding at the appointed time and there she was.

Conveniently (for him, I guess) our pastor developed laryngitis on the day of our wedding, so one of the associate pastors performed the ceremony. At this point, we were just thrilled to have someone there who was happy to make it legal. The wedding was perfect and we began our life together.

chapter 21

In July of 1980, Beth and Mike would be blessed with a son. His name was Greg and Mom was crazy about him. Her grandparenting times were limited to our visits to Tennessee, as she was not allowed to visit us. She would cherish all of the pictures they sent to her. As sisters, we made a concerted effort to travel to Tennessee with our families for Thanksgiving, so that we could be together with Mom. She would make this a Christmas celebration as well, putting up the Christmas tree and having presents for everyone. This soon became our family tradition and probably the highlight of her year.

I had told Greg when our relationship began to take a turn for the serious side that due to my injuries from the wreck, I probably would not be able to have children. The doctors had made this very clear to my mom. Greg was okay with this possibility and we began our lives together. Miraculously, I got pregnant after our first year of marriage. I miscarried at 10 weeks and we faced again the very real possibility that children might not be in our future. We moved on with our lives and 3 years later, I got pregnant. Things went smoothly with this pregnancy and in January of 1984, we had a perfect baby boy that we named Brian. When I held that baby in my arms for the first time, I knew that I would move heaven and earth if needed to protect this child. I was completely baffled how Mom could stand by and let Charles abuse us. I guess I will have to wait until I get to Heaven to ask her, but maybe then it won't matter anymore.

We continued with our annual Thanksgiving treks to Tennessee, although we could never stand to stay for very long. Charles would restrict Mom's time with us and her grandchildren. We would all be sitting around talking or playing cards and he would walk by and say, "June, come to bed." She would get up and go without a murmur.

Our visits to the ranch always included some kind of project while we were there. Charles was always one to capitalize on free labor, but we knew if it made Mom's life a little better than it was worth it. Over the years we constructed a porch on the back of the house and re-built the downstairs bathroom, wallpapering it with scripture wallpaper. (I am completely serious. We could sit on the toilet and have our devotions all at the same time.) We also remodeled the den off of the front entry that up to that point had only been used to store junk, roofed a pole shed, and one memorable Thanksgiving, we cleaned out the attic. Who knows what kind of ancient germs and dust were stirred up that day.

When our daughter, Ashley, was born in 1986, Mom couldn't wait to get her hands on her. I was discharged from the hospital on a Saturday, and they arrived just a few hours after we got home. At this point, Charles was pretty much blind and only drove by memory around the ranch. Mom had to drive the entire 8 hour trip. All she wanted to do was to hold her new granddaughter. That night, she was going to sit up and spend some time with us, when Charles told her she had to go to bed right away. He made her get up at 6 am to head back to Prospect. Their total visiting time at our house was under 14 hours.

One day, in 1988, Mom and Charles were out in the pasture trying to round up some cows to take to market to sell. Charles, of course, was riding on the tractor, while Mom was walking the pasture, trying to shoo the cows into the corral. One cow did not want to go to market and would not cooperate. She charged Mom, knocking her several feet into the air. This was during the Pentecostal / faith healing phase, so going to the hospital would have shown a lack of faith. Mom had several broken ribs and some internal injuries. She spent the next several weeks laying on the floor in their bedroom, because she was too weak to get into the bed. While she was on the floor, she was bitten multiple times by brown recluse spiders. Slowly and after many days, she was able to get up and walk again. However, the spider bites took months to heal and left huge scars on her arms and legs.

My family did have one vacation with Mom and Charles. We traveled to Florida in April of 1989 for a week's vacation. Brian was 5 years old and Ashley was 3. The condominium where we were staying was in a high rise with two bedrooms, two bathrooms and an oceanfront view. When Charles found out that the space shuttle, Atlantis, was scheduled to launch while we were there, he decided they would come. He had wanted to see a launching for many years, after his career with NASA. They had to be driven to Florida by a young couple from their church, because Mom was no longer able to drive for long distances. This poor couple had to deal with Charles' fanaticism about not filling up the gas tank until it was below a quarter of a tank. This made them very nervous, so they would just tell Charles that it was at the designated level because he could no longer see the gauge with his failing eyesight. He stumped them, though, when he asked what the total price was and how many gallons it took to fill up. Nothing but a power struggle all the way.

The four of them finally arrived and Mom was in heaven. She absolutely loved the ocean, enjoying it from the balcony and then up close and personal. Mom spent early mornings walking with Brian and Ashley on the beach picking up shells. She spent hours reading and playing with them. It was the quality Grandma time that she never had in Tennessee. Charles spent most of the time inside in the air-conditioning. We were a pretty tight fit inside the condo, but over-all, things went better than expected.

We drove out to Cape Canaveral Space Center on the appointed day to wait for the launch. We had to be there several hours early in order to get a good view. It was a hot and humid day without much to entertain two young children, and no shade to speak of. We were all excited as the final countdown moved to less than 60 seconds. The clock was suddenly stopped at 31 seconds. Talk about anticlimactic. The launch was scrubbed and rescheduled for two days later.

We returned for the second attempt in the searing heat and held our breath as the clock moved once again towards 31 seconds. Everyone was posed with hundreds of dollars of camera equipment. Greg had brought two cameras and a video camera to capture the moment. When there was liftoff, Greg's expensive camera jammed. Mom, with camera number two, had not inherited any photography genes. And I had the video camera focused on the wrong launching site. In all of the confusion, there was the rhythmic sound of a click and the winding of a manual camera. It was five year old Brian with his $4 camera, snapping away. The space shuttle quickly disappeared out of view into the clouds. Brian's pictures were the only ones that turned out. When we got back to our beachfront condo, all of our fellow vacationers who had stayed and played at the beach, kept talking about what a fantastic view they had of the space shuttle going up, all the way into the wild blue yonder. If we had only known.

chapter 22

Mom was diagnosed with lung cancer a few months later. She was a non-smoker, but over the years, she had been exposed to toxins on the crop dusters that we had refinished and tons of farm chemicals on the ranch. (Naturally, Charles' health risks were very limited because one doesn't have much exposure when one is always sitting around and thinking.) Because they had no money, Mom had to go to the Veterans Administration for her treatments. She refused surgery and chemo, agreeing only to radiation treatments. The radiation barely slowed down the spread of her cancer. My sweet prince went the extra mile so that Mom and I could do a three night cruise together that June. I had never really had one-on-one time with my mother. Coming from different states, we planned to meet up on the cruise ship. Mom flew into Miami the night before the cruise. Charles called her non-stop until she left the hotel to board the ship the next day. When we met up on board, it was as if the clock had been turned back and I got glimpses of the woman she was before

Tennessee. It was one of those one-shot opportunities. I am so very thankful that I had the chance to experience it.

That summer, our cousin, Donna Sue, Beth, Nancy and I made an extra trip home to spend some time with Mom. Nancy and I took the older kids spelunking in Cave Springs; our last trip into the cave. We planned a surprise anniversary party for Mom and Charles, a few months shy of their 25th wedding anniversary. I think Mom was touched that we would go to all the effort to plan and prepare a celebration of an event that we would just as soon mourn over. But we did it for her.

By Thanksgiving, the cancer had spread to her hips, and bones. She was in an incredible amount of pain. We made our annual Thanksgiving trek to visit her. We had tried to come up with the perfect gift for her and decided that a recliner was just the thing. She would be able to rest and put her feet up with minimal effort, as her pain was constantly increasing. We also hoped she would be able to sleep in the chair if needed. When we arrived at the ranch, we had the big box with the chair in the back of the truck. We had wrapped it and put a festive bow on it. It took some effort to get it up into the house and situated in the center of the living room. Mom was really excited about this mysterious large box. Brian, in the innocence of a five year old, asked in a very loud voice "Mommy, when is Grandma June going to open her chair?" Since the cat was out of the bag, Mom went ahead and opened her present. I think she got to sit in it for about 10 minutes before Charles settled in it and never got back up.

While we were home that November, we were really concerned about Mom. Charles would sit at the table and demand that she go upstairs to get an item or tell her to walk outside and get a random part for him. She could barely walk. She would drag one leg and cry silent tears while doing his bidding. When we offered to go for her, she would refuse. Charles never moved from the table. I had a few minutes alone with her and asked her if she would come and stay with us so we could take care of her. She looked directly into my eyes and told me that she married Charles for better or worse and she was staying with him. I have wondered where the better part came in her marriage to that man. But one thing for sure is that no one can ever say that June was a quitter. But at what price?

In 1990, during Mom's last few months, she began to tie up lose ends. She called Nancy and apologized to her for all the things that she had allowed Charles to do to her. She also told Nancy that she was finally grieving for the loss of Daddy, Raymond and Julia; twenty-six years too late. She admitted that all those years ago she had never allowed herself to weep for them.

Her two sisters made a special trip to Prospect to see her. Mom confessed to them that Charles had physically abused her over the years. She said that once a neighbor asked her how she had gotten a black-eye. She lied and told the neighbor that she had fallen against the toilet. We had suspected it, but it was so much harder to hear that she had admitted this to them. I am glad that they didn't tell us until after she died, because Charles was just not worth the prison time.

My sisters and I made multiple attempts to deliver her from Charles during her last few weeks. Beth and Nancy borrowed a custom van from a friend that had a bed in the back of it. Their plan was to get to Mom while she was at the VA hospital in Birmingham and have her discharged into their care. They had talked to the doctor in charge of Mom's case, who totally supported their plan. Somehow Charles found out about it and camped in her hospital room, refusing to leave. He would sit there, eating all of her food and prevent her from resting. The hospital staff grew to dislike him as much as we did. Beth and Nancy had to abandon their rescue attempt and return home to Oklahoma.

My family of four drove up to see Mom for Mother's Day weekend. When we got to the ranch, she and Charles were not there. Mom had gone for a doctor's appointment in Birmingham at the VA. A neighbor had driven them and when they returned, only Charles was in the car. Mom was struggling so much to breath that the doctors had admitted her to the hospital again. It was so strange to be in that house without Mom. Charles began nagging us to take him with us to Birmingham the next morning and then he wanted us to drive him back to the ranch. The drive to Birmingham was a couple of hours from Prospect and Birmingham was only about 5 hours from Greenville. Driving him back to Prospect before heading back to South Carolina would increase our travel time to 10 hours. It would also mean that we would not have any one-on-one time with Mom. We told him no, which was not well received. When we got to the VA hospital, Mom got to spend some time with us and her grandbabies without Charles controlling her visitation. Mom told us she was glad that we had left him behind.

During the last few weeks of her life, I had a sudden urgency to go and see her. Mom was back in the VA hospital and had no phone in her room. Due to the cancer, she was in too much pain to use the public phones in the hallway. Therefore, there was no way that she had any idea that I was coming. When I arrived, I walked into her hospital room. She looked at me as if she had known I was coming and said "Ellen, I am in so much pain. You have to do something." I was able to help her in small ways. She got some extra pain medication. I went to a laundromat and washed her clothes for her. I helped her wash her hair. By this time her hair was starting to fall out in big clumps. I talked her into letting me cut a few inches off of it so that it wouldn't be such a mess. And that was the last time I got to see her, hug her and tell her how much I loved her.

chapter 23

From the day they married, Charles methodically drained away all of Mom's financial independence. He deliberately moved her away from her support system. By the end of her life, she didn't even have health insurance and had to use her VA benefits for health care. He abused her physically, psychologically and emotionally for the 25 years they were married. He also severed her relationship with her mother and attempted to dissect her from her daughters. By the time Charles had finished expanding his ranch, he had about 1200 acres. He never seemed to have any workable plans to actually do anything with the land; it was more about the bragging rights of owning over 1,000 acres. Charles was a master manipulator. He extinguished the joy in life. Everything he touched turned to crap. He was an abuser and a user.

I got the phone call in the early morning hours abruptly telling me that Mom had died on June 11th, 1990. She had died in her sleep, bless her heart;

heaven knows she needed the rest. But the ordeal didn't end with her death.

When it came to funerals, Mom was a bare bones kind of girl (pun intended). She wanted to be cremated and have a simple service. She had already paid for a marker to be placed in Pennsylvania on Daddy, Ray and Julia's headstone. But Charles was determined to do it his way. Perhaps it was his constant need to be the center of attention, or maybe it was his last chance to spite her. He planned a full-blown funeral with everything she hated; the open casket; the waste of flowers, the church service, the cemetery plot, and the ridiculously large monstrosity of a headstone. Mom would have the last laugh, though.

The funeral was in the middle of June and the temperatures were in the triple digits. None of us felt comfortable staying in the house now that Mom was gone. We booked rooms at a hotel in Pulaski. The service was held at the Church of the Living Savior with no air conditioning. The church was packed with people from the community who came to show their respect. The grandkids were pretty young and all this was a new and frightening thing for them. We had tried to think of some symbolic way to share with them that Grandma wasn't really there; it was just her shell. We picked up some white helium balloons that morning and kept them in the car for the graveside service. By the time we got into the car to drive to the cemetery, the balloons were starting to fade due to the heat and humidity. The minister paused during the service and explained what we had planned for the grandchildren. We gave each of them a balloon to release as a symbol of Grandma June's spirit floating up to heaven. The problem was that the balloons weren't going to float anywhere. They kept dropping back to the ground. The kids quickly got into the spirit and started kicking the balloons to try to launch them. Greg tried to lighten the load by shortening the ribbons on the balloons. In the absence of a pocket knife, he resorted to "sawing" the ribbons off on a nearby headstone. I am sure that the local folks whose "people" were buried in this cemetery were appalled by his desecration of the headstones. The balloons were dead, so to speak, and we had to take them away from the kids before they began trying to pop them.

After a few more minutes of inspirational words, a drone of an airplane could be heard coming our way. One of Mom's pilot friends had wanted to circle the gravesite during the ceremony and drop out carnations as a tribute to her. It was a sweet gesture, but the reality was a little hard to endure. After the plane circled several times, we could see objects falling from above. There was little warning before we began to get pelted with carnations from the sky. It felt like hail when they hit. People were scurrying around trying to get out of target range.

After the burial, Charles made a big presentation about reading Mom's will while everyone was at the house within hours of the funeral. Basically she left all of her money (not that there was any left) to Charles. However, she specified that all of the furniture and items that she had brought from Pennsylvania were to be divided among the three of us girls. She had carefully listed each piece. These items were really important to Nancy. Many of them had been passed down through our family for several generations. And some of them were pieces of furniture that Daddy had lovingly made so many years before.

Charles decided that he had to order the biggest headstone to be made for Mom's gravesite. Of course, his money train was gone, so he sent out letters to all the people on Mom's Christmas list asking for donations. I bet Mom was doing 360's in her casket. Several months later when the headstone arrived, it was to my delight to find out from a friend that they had misspelled Charles' name on the headstone. It was missing an "h" where it said "Beloved wife of Charles Meager..." (Not M-E-A-G-_H_-E-R). Mom really did have the last laugh.

chapter 24

About a month after Mom died, Beth and Nancy rented a moving truck and headed up to Tennessee to get the items left to us in the will. Charles was unhappy about this, to say the least. The more items that they placed into the truck, the more agitated he became. Beth and Nancy were trying to pack up the truck and get back on the road as fast as possible. When they started to load up the kitchen table (which was a family heirloom), Charles really began to unravel. He lost it and headed upstairs where the guns were kept. Beth and Nancy were feeling very unsafe at this point. They were convinced that Charles was going to kill them. At that very moment, in the miraculous timing of God, a car drove up to the house at 1:00 in the morning. It was a young man who attended Charles' church. His presence totally diffused the situation. It is amazing who God can use as a guardian angel. Beth and Nancy wasted no time in closing up the truck and getting out of town. They didn't take a good deep breath until they had crossed over the state line.

During this quick stop in Prospect, Charles had casually mentioned to Beth and Nancy that he was still getting life insurance checks in Mom's name and cashing them, even though she was dead. He assured them that Mom would want him to have this money. When Beth got back to Tulsa, she pulled up the information. The money was a monthly payout from a life insurance policy of our Dad's. She notified the insurance company of Mom's death and the remaining funds were divided among the three of us. There wasn't much left, but it was something for us from our Dad. Charles was irate and declared that the insurance money would be the last thing we would receive. And it was.

That summer, in August, the three of us planned a memorial service for our Mom in Pennsylvania, with all of her relatives and friends. It was a sweet time of remembering and just what Mom would have wanted. We each took turns sharing with these special people what had been happening with Mom the last 25 years. Her three grandchildren even had a part in the service. Afterwards, we walked down the hill to visit the marker for Daddy, Raymond and Julia. Soon, Mom's name would be added with theirs, just as she had wanted. Charles was not invited to this event and he was not missed in any way.

chapter 25

In 1994, Nancy was turning the big 4-0. Beth and I flew to Oklahoma to celebrate her birthday with her. What a nice birthday present it was to get the phone call while we were there that Charles had died. His death was a bit suspicious; he was found dead in the bathroom with a large knot on his head and all the money from a recent sale of a bulldozer was missing. But no one seemed to care enough to want to investigate. It was such an emotional relief to know that he could no longer cause us any more grief or pain.

During their last years, Charles and Mom were befriended by a strange family. The best way to describe these people is that they were hangers-on. These people wormed their way into every aspect of Mom and Charles' lives. They attended their church and even lived at the house for a time. Charles made this couple the executors of his will. There were some oil shares that had been handed down through the Meagher family for several generations. Charles named this couple as guardians of these shares for his three children. They were to keep the money in trust and when they decided that Charles' kids were "worthy" then they were to pass the shares and profits on to them. Of course they decided early on that his children would never be "worthy" and they proceeded to use these proceeds that were not theirs to spend. They were also named the beneficiaries of the few paltry life insurance policies that Charles had, and then didn't want to pay for his burial costs. They supervised the auction of the farm and everything in it, and this money was never accounted for. Someday, somewhere, there will be an accounting for this game of life.

In 1996, my family and I traveled to Tennessee for my twentieth high school reunion. We went back to Prospect for a final look around. The ranch and house had been sold off in an auction after Charles had died. A few months later, the house on the hill mysteriously burned to the ground. After they were unable to determine the cause of the fire, the new owner had hired a bulldozer to get rid of the charred remains.

We climbed over the gate and walked up what had once been the driveway. At the top of the hill, I stood still and surveyed the place that had taken such a long time to escape from. The airplane hangers and other out-buildings were still visible, but had tangled vines and weeds weaving around them as they reclaimed their place. But the house and the swimming pool were completely erased. It was as if they had never even existed. I was overcome with a cleansing feeling because they had symbolized such a tumultuous time in my life. Then I was struck with the irony as I realized that Mom had tunneled all of her livelihood into that property; all of her blood, sweat and tears; and there was absolutely nothing left. All that Charles had treasured was returned to God's green earth. I wasn't even aware that I was crying, until I felt a tear fall from my cheek. I bent down and dug around in the dirt trying to find something from our past. I managed to unearth three bricks. One for each of us…. survivors….. strong women…. moving on with life. It has been said that what doesn't kill you, makes you stronger. We are some damn strong women.

epilogue

june

As we go through life, we want to believe that we are independent individuals on our own private road. The reality is that we are all swimming in a big pond and in many respects, we are connected together. When a rock hits one of us, the ripples spread out across the surface and we all feel the vibrations. Choose wisely in life. This ain't no dress rehearsal; it is the real thing.

Dear Mom,

As I have worked my way through all of the many feelings and emotions of putting these events and memories on paper, I have shed many tears. Many times I was so mad at you that if I'd had a phone line to Heaven, I would have called you and asked you "Why?" Why did you fail us so completely? Why did you uproot us from a happy and secure place? Why did you marry a stranger and drop us into the cesspool that was his world? Why didn't you walk away when you saw how crazy he was? Why didn't you just run over the bastard with a tractor and pretend it was an accident? No one would have questioned it. Most would have applauded it. I would have cheered.

I guess until you walk in someone else's shoes, you can't appreciate the burdens they carry. If you had only allowed yourself to grieve when we lost our family. We would have understood and admired you more for it. Our lives would have been so different if you hadn't married that man. But we can't sit around and cry over what might have been.

We are three strong women as a result of the fires that we went through; Steel Magnolias, if you will. We have looked death in the face many times and survived. We lived with the devil and still walked away with a strong and enduring love for God. As a result of your poor choice the second time around, we have chosen kind and caring men; sweet princes. We have made an extra effort to be the kind of parents that we did not have. We have encouraged our kids and told them that we believe in them and they can do great and wonderful things. And they have! It is amazing how things can grow with a little sunshine and love.

I regret that you didn't outlive the scoundrel so that you could have had the relationship with each of us that he didn't allow. I hope that you are finally happy. I pray that you are free from pain and that Grandma Jones, Daddy, Raymond and Julia were there to welcome you when you crossed over the Jordan. I look forward to knowing we will all be together one day and there will be no more tears or regrets.

After all of this, I want to tell you that I love you. I know that you stayed with Charles out of pride. You had always been the overachiever and had never failed at anything. You just couldn't admit to the world that the whole thing had been a terrible mistake and walk away. But we learned from your mistakes, and maybe that is what marriage and parenting is all about: trying to be better than the imperfect parents that we had.

Until I see you again, God bless you. Take care. And don't let the bedbugs bite tonight.
Love,
Ellen Lee

Made in the USA
Columbia, SC
13 April 2021